OUR ENDURING HERITAGE

THE LIFE OF A
NORWEGIAN-AMERICAN
FAMILY

ROALD G. LUND

"… The fragile, heroic enterprise of remembering … that basic human task … Deciding to remember, and what we remember, is how we decide who we are."

— Robert Pinsky, Poet Laureate of the United States

OUR ENDURING HERITAGE. Copyright © 2000 by Roald G. Lund. All rights reserved. Printed in the United States of America. No part of this book may be used or reproduced in any manner watsoever, except for the inclusion of brief quotations in a review, without written permission from the author..

For information, address Roald G. Lund, 15315 SW Bull Mountain Road, Tigard, Oregon 97224 USA.

FIRST EDITION

Lund, Roald G., 1912 -
Our Enduring Heritage: The Life of a Norwegian-American Family / Roald G. Lund — 1st ed.

ISBN 0-9707282-0-4

For Gunnar and Marie.

With special gratitude to Helga
for her encouragement, prodding, help
and her wonderful enthusiasm
that sustained me through the long ordeal
of fact gathering and writing.

CONTENTS

INTRODUCTION

Heritage. Is it real? Is it desirable? What does it consist of? How and where do we find it and what do we do with it?

These are a few of the topics this book probes in recounting the lives of two Norwegian immigrants who met in the United States and settled in Seattle at the beginning of the twentieth century. An important part of the story is the Norwegian-language newspaper that became the cornerstone of their lives. Through its pages we are also able to open a window in time to view the lives of Norwegian-Americans on the Pacific Coast. We also follow the immigrants' three children as they mature and a final chapter explores the meaning and benefits of heritage and the special heritage the newspaper editor left his children.

* * *

When we three children of Gunnar and Marie Lund were small, we assumed all families were like ours. But as we grew older, we learned that our family was "different" – first, our parents were Norwegian. We learned it was almost impossible for neighbor children to understand that our father was the editor of a Norwegian-language newspaper. "What is *that*?" they asked, and we found it very difficult to explain. Furthermore, our mother was rarely at home every day like most mothers in the neighborhood; she was so often away at a meeting or, if home, busy planning some program for one of the Norwegian organizations.

In those early days we did not know that Father's life work had been a serious balancing act between success and failure. As his experience grew, publishing his newspaper was still at times a numbing routine with endless change and an endless cycle of starting and finishing; one weekly newspaper was fresh from the press when he had to start work on the next week's edition. That was one of the reasons he always brought work home for most of his evening hours. And he, like Mother, was also active in a number of Norwegian organizations.

His life itself was a continuous mingling of loyalties. There was the United States — land of liberty, land of promise, land of democracy, land of Lincoln and, also, the land of Gunnar's own choice. Gunnar was both delighted and proud to be an American citizen. Also, there was always Norway — beautiful, remembered, beloved, off there in the distance, the ever-beckoning land of the fjords and "home," the land of the Eidsvoll men who had given Norway its first constitution and thereby established the national Seventeenth of May holiday, celebrated by Norwegians wherever they might live around the world.

There was the English, for Father a new language. He mastered it through need and painstaking persistence; and there was Norwegian, the changing language of today, and his lifetime favorite study, Old Norse, the language of the sagas.

We never thought of him as a series of strange dichotomies — vibrant Americanism on one side and, just as fervently, a deep, continuing interest in Norway. While he was certainly unlike the fathers of our young friends, we did admire him, accepting him as being the way a father should be. We all looked forward to getting to know his Norway. That is something he made happen, and we were grateful when we experienced it.

We understood his work was no pathway to wealth. He made that plain through his response when our mother handed him a grocery or department store bill that had come in the mail. His reaction was predictably one of irritation and accusation. That, too, seemed completely natural. So did the fact that Mother never appeared to be concerned. She knew there was never enough money. Rugs might go threadbare too long. Children's need for shoes might come more often than they could be afforded. That might have been important to her, but she never showed it.

She had a richly busy life of her own. She gave of her time and her plentiful talents to a number of organizations. Even as a young woman and all through her adult life she gladly accepted responsibility for leadership and demonstrated her capabilities through unflagging work and bountiful creativity. . She frequently wrote articles for her husband's newspaper, especially in her later days. And she never forgot that she was a mother and homemaker.

He was Gunnar Lund. By his own choice he had no middle name. She was Marie Vognild Lund; Vognild was her maiden name and harked back to the high farm valley of Oppdal in Norway

The communities in which Marie and Gunnar existed were both far-flung and constricted. They became personages in Norway long after they were widely known in large stretches of the United States. But it was a selective public here – mainly a Norwegian-American public over the entire West Coast although both of them had acquaintances, friends, and even admirers among non-hyphenated Americans.

Time passed. Gunnar and Marie became remembered figures of a receding yesterday. All three children had moved from Seattle: John to North Carolina, Helga to Florida, and I to Oregon.

Fifty years after Gunnar's death I received a telephone call from a stranger. That call switched on a few months of hectic activity that tapered off into almost nine years of gnawing inaction and finally caused the present long months of sustained work, the fact-finding and writing of this book. Looking back, I now know I should have thanked the caller. If he had not called me, my sister and I might never have started what we both knew should be done. If we didn't undertake the task, it would never be done for nobody else was left to do it.

There was no question about my caller's nationality. I could tell it by his accent and the way he pronounced my name, how he rolled the R, broadened the O, accented the first syllable and kept the D's silent. I wondered what this unknown Norwegian wanted of me.

"Is this Roald Lund?" he asked.

"Yes," I answered.

"I am Capt. Gunnar Olsborg, " he announced. "I am gathering information on Norwegian pioneers for the Nordic Heritage Museum here in Seattle. Do you have anything in writing about your parents that you could send me?"

"No," I responded, feeling quite guilty, and then added, "but I think my sister Helga and I could get something together in a fairly short time."

He thanked me warmly, gave me his mailing address and spelled out his name for me. He didn't really need to spell his first name, it was Gunnar, a name I will never forget. I looked at my watch. Eleven o'clock in Florida, that was far beyond bedtime and much too late to call my sister there.

The call went through the following morning.

Within a few weeks we sent Capt. Olsborg an article and photos. He was delighted, but we were disappointed. There was too much we did not know. Some weeks later the May 4, 1990 edition of *Western Viking,* the weekly Norwegian-American newspaper came from Seattle. We were surprised and pleased to find a full page devoted to our article and the pictures with an explanatory box:

> *This story should, of course, have been included in our 100th anniversary issue, published May 17, 1989. However, I was not able to get this story until recently.*
>
> *Captain Gunnar Olsborg, who has made an effort to secure stories about well-known persons within our Norwegian colony in Seattle 50 or more years back in time, brought this story and pictures to Western Viking's office. The material was to be turned over to the Norwegian Room in Nordic Heritage Museum, for display he said, but he thought it also might be of interest to the newspaper where Mr. Lund spent 33 years of his life as publisher.*
>
> *We hope that at least those of our subscribers who read Washington Posten 50 years ago will remember one or both of these fine, dedicated Norwegian-Americans, — and enjoy reading this resume of their services to further the Norwegian heritage in America.*
>
> *Henning C. Boe*
> *Publisher and Editor of*
> *Western Viking the last 31 years*

The article covered only the essential information on our parents: where they came from and some of what they both contributed as Norwegian-Americans to their fellow countrymen and to the colorful fabric that is the United

States. Years after Gunnar's death his newspaper was eventually purchased by Henning Boe, a recent Norwegian immigrant, who changed the paper's name to *Western Viking*. In keeping with the times, he also changed its language from almost exclusively Norwegian to mostly English.

Three weeks after our story appeared in *Western Viking* I was on my way from Portland to North Carolina and Florida. During the long plane ride I scribbled questions to put to my brother John in Chapel Hill and Helga in Naples. For several hours I grilled John, holding the microphone close to catch every soft-spoken word as he contributed dates and key facts and wonderful reminiscences, but at age eighty-eight and in failing health, it was clear we could not count on his active involvement.

Helga had many vivid memories, enthusiasm and ambitious plans for collaboration in producing a fitting memorial to the parents we considered so deserving. We quickly agreed that even if we had to publish it ourselves, we *would* write a book. That was the debt we owed our parents, our children, our grandchildren and our great grandchildren. And maybe, just maybe, in the process of the necessary research and writing of the book, we would also find an answer to a puzzle Father had left us.

John recalled something father had said to him many years before when John was in his middle twenties and was about to leave for a year of graduate studies in Norway.

"John," Father began, "I think you know I won't be able to leave you children any money. There won't be any inheritance. But we are leaving you a rich heritage."

John nodded, "You mean our being Norwegian."

"Yes, that too," Gunnar had replied. "But there's much more than that. It's something you will understand when you are older." Then, putting an end to the conversation,

"Have a good year in Norway. I will be waiting to hear from you."

When John told me of this, I asked him if he had talked about that rich heritage matter any further. "No," John replied, "I never did. Funny, I knew he assumed that I understood him fully and I was afraid to show that I didn't. That was almost sixty years ago. I guess I felt it was some kind of sentimental thing about our relationship with Norway. In my mind it was a foggy idea, something like what most Norwegian-Americans think of as heritage."

I saw John just once after that meeting in Chapel Hill. At that time I again asked if he had been able to define what our father had meant regarding the word "heritage."

John was now just a year away from his 90th birthday. He laughed. "No, I don't really have a clue. You might call it a 'hidden heritage.' And it obviously is much more than just Norwegian things – you know, much more than just *lutefisk*, *lefse* and the Seventeenth of May. It must have been something more, even something different than that."

Over the next few months my sister Helga and I were in constant touch by letter and phone as we gathered information and probed our own memories for details our parents had told us about their lives.

I suggested one theme of the book would be solving the problem of defining the "heritage" John had told us about. She agreed, "That would be great, if we can ever solve the puzzle."

The data gathering continued until my increasingly heavy client workload put longer and longer gaps in the book project. It languished, and though it frequently gave me pangs of conscience, it finally died. Helga and I still talked regularly on the phone, but when she asked if I was doing any writing, I had to admit that I simply had no time for it. After I retired at 83 (officially, if not fully) my story changed.

Now, I complained, I was getting too old to do any orderly thinking, let alone writing.

Then, as summer was turning into early fall in 1999, something snapped. For no good reason and without any dire need, I bought a new Macintosh laptop computer. It went along with me on a week in our cabin at the ocean where I started playing with this new toy. When I returned to Tigard I called Helga, who was now 93. "Guess what," I told her, "I'm sending you a chapter-by chapter-synopsis. I've started on the first chapter!"

What follows is what we discovered about those two early immigrants, our parents, and what problems they faced, what they made of their lives as Americans, and especially, how Gunnar fared in the new profession he reluctantly undertook in 1905. One situation was inescapable, the long years it had taken Gunnar to find his real life's work: being the editor and publisher of *Washington Posten*, the Seattle Norwegian-language newspaper. He purchased it knowing it had gone through a series of owners and editors and had become, as some called it, "a white elephant." He bought it fearing he too might fail. He could not know how well he would do. He did not anticipate how that newspaper would change him and influence his entire family. The newspaper he edited for thirty-three years and the widespread immigrant community it served became one major theme of the story.

Rather than a lean recital of happenings, I chose to put the story into narrative form. All the events really occurred. All the people mentioned are real. Fortunately, there were many reliable sources of information and the *Washington Posten* files for those thirty-three years were the greatest single source. A list of all sources is given at the end of the book. Our parents and our relatives in the United States and Norway told us many of the situations reported. I am aware that memories can be fallible as to precise details on dates, names, places and who said what to whom. I had to create some of the quoted remarks, drawing on memory of how our parents said things and what they told us of long ago events. In a very few instances where documentation was not available, that is so reported and the cause is given.

This then is the story of a Norwegian-American family and of a weekly Norwegian-American newspaper, its dedicated editor, his talented wife and their three children. It is an immigrant story that at the very end does indeed discover the meaning of the heritage Gunnar and Marie left us, a heritage so many immigrants left to enrich the lives of so many American descendants.

Chapter 1

MARIE

Oppdal is at once a mountain valley, a town, and a way of life. Many of the farms, and this is true for those that will be mentioned here, go back in time more than six hundred years. The name Oppdal means "high valley." It lies in the mountains of central Norway about two hour drive from Trondheim and a stop on the Oslo-Trondheim railway that climbs through the Dovre mountain range with its striking scenery and high plateaus. Though we are speaking of a bygone day, we use the modern spelling "Trondheim" for the 900-year-old city that was formerly spelled Trondhjem and we also use Oppdal, the modern spelling for Opdal.

The river Driva divides the Oppdal valley. On the north side the main road runs westward past the church and a farm called *Gulsenget* (The Golden Field), where the Dørum family lives. Beyond that lies a hamlet named Vognill – the newer spelling of Vognild. There is a cluster of large farms there, one of them the main Vognild farm. Further west lies the viking-age burial ground of Vang, dating back to about the year 500.

By the year 1000 it is estimated there were about 40 farms in Oppdal. Across the Driva near the east end and on the south side of the valley is the Viken farm. In its forested lower area there are massive clumps of granite. In one of these a discovery was made during the 1920's of a very large natural cave with artifacts indicating that the farm family had lived there during the wars that raged through this peaceful valley many centuries before.

The Viken, Vognild and Dørum farms and the families who lived there played a major part in Marie's life. For us three Norwegian-Americans it was the Viken and the Dørum farms that we called "our family farms." Marie's American children all made repeated pilgrimages to these farms, as Marie herself did. We owed so much to the farmers of these two places who in about 1883 left the pressing work of the spring farm season to make the long trip in to the city of Trondheim. Their mission was to bring Marie and her sister and brother back to the Oppdal families after their voyage west and south to Norway from northern Russia.

Their father, Johannes Larsen Vognild, had learned the watch-making and goldsmith trade from his father, who was a watchmaker as well as a farmer. This was normal in many parts of Norway; the men learned a trade to bring cash to the farm. It was also common for the younger sons to leave the farm, for under the primogeniture law the first-born son inherited the farm.

Johannes had another brother named Erik Lars Vognild, also a watchmaker, who struck out first to establish himself in Troms County north of the Arctic Circle. After Johannes left Oppdal, he went to join his brother in Troms. Having heard of the fast growth of Vardø, then the largest city in all of Finnmark County, Johannes left for that island city on the eastern tip of northern Norway, far north of the Arctic Circle and almost at the Russian border.

It was in Vardø that Johannes met and married Eva Pauline Sophie Sand. She was ten years younger than Johannes and had come to Vardø with her widowed father

Johannes and Eva Vognild with their children, Marie, Leonard and Anna, dressed for their move to Archangel, Russia — Vardø, Norway 1875.

mesterskomaker (master shoemaker) and guild member Didrik Johannes Christian Sand. His wife Marie Amesdatter Olestad Sand died while the family lived in Hammerfest, another far northern city. Didrik remarried in Vardø. Since he came there and apparently departed between census takings, he left no trace. Nor is there any record of where Eva's mother was born in Norway. The Vardø church records for those years were destroyed in a fire, so there is no record of exactly when Johannes and Eva were married but family correspondence sets the date at "about" 1869. The couple had three children: Marie Pauline who was born in 1870, Leonard in 1872, and Anna Dorotea in 1874.

Johannes had written letters to his family in Oppdal after the boy was born and two years later a typical farm-made wooden chest came from the home farm, Vognild. It contained clothing for Marie and Leonard. The chest had wrought iron handles and a massive iron key for the farm-made lock. It was newly painted in typical *rosemaling* style and dated "Year 1873" – the year of the painting. But the method of construction and the smithing of the iron hinges, lock, key and studding made it easy for Johannes to identify. It had probably come to Vognild with the trousseau of one of the young women who married into the family in the early 1700's or possibly the late 1600's. The old chest's history would not end in Vardø.

In a few years Johannes heard from his brother that he now felt there would never be real opportunity for him in the Troms area so he was going to Chicago in "Amerika" hoping it would be a better place to set up a business. That it certainly was. Erik became a prominent watchmaker and jeweler there.

Johannes stuck it out in cold, barren, windswept Vardø for another year. Vardø was the major Norwegian port in the *pomor* trade with Russians who lived along the coast by the village of Murmansk and along the shores of the White Sea as far east as the major city of Archangel.

Pomor is a Russian word meaning "by the sea." On any given day there would be from 10 to 20 large and small Russian sailing ships in Vardø harbor, some bringing grain, some bringing cod liver or cod liver oil, some with timber. Much of the *pomor* trade was barter, especially for large halibut or dried cod called *klippfisk*, but the Russian traders also sold some goods for Norwegian *kroner*, which they then spent on Norwegian goods, including watches and watch repair.

Most of the Norwegian merchants, including those of

Я ЛЕЙЦИНГЕРЪ   АРХАНГЕЛЬСКЪ

*Marie Pauline Vognild
at age 12 — Archangel,
Russia 1887.*

the large trading firms as well as Johannes, learned to speak a little Russian. He heard from his customers, both Russians and Norwegians, of the very large city at the southeastern end of the White Sea, Archangel. Johannes investigated. Archangel was far larger than Vardø and growing much faster. He had proved to himself that there was little chance of major success for him in Vardø. Johannes saw and chatted with Russian *pomor* people almost every day, He knew that quite a number of Norwegians from Vardø had crossed the open border and were living in various Russian towns in the Murmansk area, and that there were numerous

Norwegians living in Archangel. The Russian port was thus no strange, foreign city to Johannes. It was a neighboring city with close trade and personal bonds to Vardø. Perhaps, he thought, this was the place where some years of work could give him the success he so eagerly sought.

Johannes, Eva and their three children left Norway for Archangel. Johannes did extremely well. The family lived in a fine house. The children had a Russian governess who taught them Russian, German and a little French; the Norwegian language was little used in their home.

Johannes wrote to his brother in Chicago: "Now, I, too, am beginning to find real success. My question is which of us will have the biggest business by 1890?"

But Archangel was to be a city of tragedy for the family. The children's mother died. In later years her children called it pneumonia, but they had strong reasons to suspect that Eva died of tuberculosis. It was a dreaded disease, for in those years there was no cure and people talked of it in hushed tones. A year after Eva's funeral Johannes died.

It is assumed that letters must have come from the Norwegian Consul in Archangel to Johannes' sisters, Dordi (Vognild) Viken, the mistress of the Viken farm and Marit (Vognild) Dørum, mistress of the Dørum farm. The letters told the sad story of the death of Johannes and his wife Eva, and that the three children would be put aboard the Norwegian freighter *Arkangelsk* which should arrive in Trondheim with a load of Russian lumber on a date early in June. A hurried letter had been written to the children's uncle Erik Vognild in Chicago and he had promptly replied that he would gladly take two of the children.

There are questions to which there are no answers: How did the Norwegian Consul get the names of Dordi Viken and Marit Dørum? Possibly Johannes, on his deathbed, told him.

Possibly he found in Johannes' home letters from Dordi and Marit. Who packed the essential clothing for the voyage into the old red-painted chest and saw that it accompanied the children aboard the ship *Arkangelsk?* There is no way to know.

It was probably a ten-day voyage on the cramped vessel. Seagoing freighters of that period were not built for crew comfort and certainly not for the comfort of three children ranging from nine to thirteen years. But Capt. Espesen and his crew all but adopted the children and made the voyage a memorable experience. The men were especially taken with twelve-year-old Leonard, and "because he was a man" they brought him up to the command bridge when they were coming in to Trondheim. He stood there in his light blue sailor's suit watching the ship slowly ease its way to the dock.

The children had been told that relatives from Oppdal would be waiting on the dock. Marie who was thirteen was excited with the thought of meeting real relatives. She could dimly remember her mother's father who had left Vardø even before the Vognild family went to Russia. She had made sure that her nine-year-old sister Anna wore her best dress and at the last moment tied bows on her braids. Marie had on her prettiest dress and was carrying her blue and black hat. She and her sister Anna stood by the rail as the ship slowly came in to the dock. She saw a slender dark-haired man on the dock looking directly at her and waving. It was Erik Viken who had made the two-day trip by wagon and train from Oppdal to Trondheim. By his side was his brother-in-law Knut Dørum. When Marie waved back at Erik he smiled broadly and turned to his friend saying, "That one, the oldest, holding her hat, she is surely one of them. It's not hard to know that she and the little one are Vognilds. They *look* like Vognilds."

After the ship had tied up at the dock, the Captain took the three children down the gangplank where Erik and Knut were waiting. Captain Espesen looked at the two men quizzically and Erik introduced himself, "Captain, I am Erik Viken, the children's uncle and this is Knut Dørum, also an uncle to the children. We thank you for taking such good care of them."

The Captain replied, "And I thank you for coming. I couldn't just give these fine children to anyone."

Erik, Knut and the children spent a few days in Trondhjem where they went to see the famous old medieval Nidaros Cathedral that dates from the year 1070. For the children, the big treat was the visit to the city square. They liked to look at the fruits and vegetables and all the good things to eat. The children stopped to admire the breads one old woman was selling, and they told her they thought they might be going to America.

"Amerika!" she exclaimed, "Then you had better play a lot here in Norway because no one has time to play in Amerika." The children looked at each other. So that was how it was in America!

On the way to Oppdal they were fascinated by the train ride to Støren and equally pleased with the wagon and horse which Erik had left there. At the stage stop at Garli in the Sokne valley they stayed the night. The next day Marie saw to it that the old red chest was placed in the bed of the wagon so the girls could sit on it while Leonard sat between the two uncles on the driver's seat. At the end of the many hour wagon trip they stopped first at Dørum farm. There, Marit greeted the travelers and reported she had seen Dordi Viken at church and they had agreed that Anna would stay for now at Dørum. Marie opened the old chest and handed Anna's clothing to Marit. Then the chest was closed again and lifted into the wagon bed. Erik helped Marie and Leonard up to the driver's seat and they started the hour-long trip back up the valley and across to Viken farm.

To the children, the Viken house appeared to be much like the Dørum house; It was a long two-story building in typical Oppdal style. It had an inviting doorway and wide slate steps and porch. The log walls of Norway pine were burned deep reddish brown by the sun. The house looked out over the field to the woods below and across the valley. On the slate porch stood a woman, wiping her hands on her apron and waiting to greet the children.

It was Dordi of Viken. She invited the children into the large farm kitchen where she served them milk and small cakes. Then she showed them to their rooms on the second story and Erik carried up the old chest.

None of the children spoke Norwegian with any ease, but Marie did seem to understand a little. Dordi found it hard to communicate with them at first but this eased during their three-month stay.

After the arrival of the children Dordi wrote her brother Erik in Chicago to tell him the children were now in Oppdal. Erik had agreed to take the two girls and now sent tickets. Within a few weeks arrangements had been made with a friend of the family who was going back to America. He was to shepherd the children on the long trip to Chicago – by wagon and train to Trondheim, ship to England, another ship to New York and rail to Chicago. No one knows why the Vikens sent Marie and her brother Leonard instead of sending the two girls as Erik Vognild had requested. Nor can anyone explain why little Anna was not told until the next morning that her brother and sister were on their way to America. When she heard the news she threw herself on the floor, kicking and crying, Speaking of it years later when she met her sister Marie again, Anna said, "I can't tell you how broken- hearted I was, I thought you two had forgotten me and left me behind."

The two children arrived in Chicago in September 1883 and joined the growing family of Erik and Amalie Vognild where there were already seven children. Young Leonard died a year later, but Marie, then fourteen, became one of the family.

Amalie taught Marie to sew, and soon Marie was helping her aunt make clothes for her younger cousins. Within a short time she became the dressmaker of the family. When she turned 18, Marie became a live-in governess in the wealthy Dwight home, taking care of the two little daughters and, to the delight of Mrs. Dwight, making them dresses.

Agnes Dwight quickly noticed Marie's aptitude. As she told her husband, "Marie does not need a pattern, she just drapes the fabric on a child and starts cutting, the pattern is in her head. And what comes out of her work is so stylish, so unusual. She has an amazing natural talent."

Two years later Mrs. Dwight paid for Marie's tuition at the S. T. Taylor School of Dress Design. Marie was a star pupil there. She began designing and sewing dresses for Mrs. Dwight. Before Marie turned 21, Mrs. Dwight helped in financing the dressmaking establishment Marie opened in the fashionable suburban city of Evanston.

Within a year, Marie had seamstresses working for her. In those days, fabrics were expensive, heavy brocades. Marie continued to work without patterns. Her customers came to the shop, were helped in selecting a fabric, and Marie designed in her head, draped and cut. And the business grew. At its peak there were twenty seamstresses working in her shop.

Marie was delighted with her good fortune, for it made possible seeing her sister Anna again, not by going to Norway but by bringing Anna from Norway to Evanston twice. The bond between the two was close, and they deeply enjoyed being together.

In the fall of 1897 it was time for the trip Marie had been planning for years. The only ship that met her own schedule was the tiny Tingvalla that took two weeks to cross from New York to London. Marie was on her way "home" to Norway and would not return to Evanston until the late summer of 1898.

Her first stop was one of several long visits with her younger sister Anna at the village of Brekstad on the fjord west of Trondheim. Anna had attended a school for teachers in Oppdal, and it is thought Uncle Erik in Chicago financed this. Later she moved to Brekstad where she taught school. The two sisters spent hours telling each other of their experiences. They bicycled to famous old Austråt castle, a stately monument to the egotism of a medieval nobleman. The bicycling created a stir in Brekstad where both the men and women were mildly scandalized by the unladylike spectacle of young women on bicycles. They went sailing with Simon Wiggen, the handsome young bank cashier Anna married in 1902, with services held in the stately Nidaros Cathedral in Trondheim.

Marie Vognild, the Norwegian orphan whose parents had died in Archangel, Russia at last had the opportunity to see the Norway she had never really known. She saw a great deal of it, and the Norway she had heard so much about at last became *her* Norway. She loved it all, especially the home area of her father's people, Oppdal.

Erik Viken and Knut Dørum had met her when she came from Russia on the freighter *Arkangelsk*. Now they were both at the Oppdal station to greet her on her return visit to Norway. Erik drove her out to Viken in a new wagon he had made during the previous winter. They came up the long curving road through the woods and the big field. The barley was ripening well and almost ready for harvesting, there was smoke curling out of the main chimney in the big farmhouse. And on the slate porch Dordi, Erik's wife, was waiting.

Once inside they must have the ritual coffee and small cakes, but not in the kitchen. Marie was ushered into the parlor dining room reserved for very special guests. This was an occasion; the farm people were greeting a finely dressed American lady who once had been the young orphan who came to them from Russia.

Dordi and Erik asked about the Chicago Vognilds and how Anna was doing at Brekstad. After the second cup of coffee and the third small cake, Marie held up her hand and said that she wanted to change into simpler clothes. Dordi took her up the steep curved stairway to her room, Erik following with Marie's baggage. As they reached the second floor, Marie stopped and exclaimed, "The old chest!"

There it was, against the far wall, still bearing the 1873 date, the chest that had come north to Vardø, then to Archangel, then by ship down to Trondheim and with the children to Oppdal.

"When you went to America we never thought to send it with you," Dordi explained. "Erik put it away and just brought it out this morning as a surprise for you. Will you want to take it with you when you leave, as a reminder of your parents and Norway?"

Marie nodded, brushing aside her tears, and held Dordi close for a moment. When she left three days later, the chest was in the buggy with her, and it followed her back to Brekstad where she took her sister Anna with her to England and New York with the old red chest accompanying them as baggage.

In England they boarded the largest ship in the Cunard Line fleet, the palatial Campania which took less than a week to make the crossing. But when they were going through customs in New York the chest could not be found. In a panic,

Marie and Anna went back aboard the ship and complained of the loss. The ship's baggage master was called, a gentleman who was well used to calming upset passengers. He bowed slightly, "Miss Vognild, I am dreadfully sorry but we can't seem to find your trunk anywhere. It seems to have disappeared into thin air. If you could just describe the trunk to me..."

"But it *isn't* a trunk," she interrupted. "It's about a meter long, half a meter wide, maybe a little over half a meter high with a slightly rounded top, and it's painted a darkish red with black and white trim, a yellow and blue flower and the year 1873 painted on it and there's a very large keyhole."

The baggage master's eyes lit up. *"It's a chest... a wooden immigrant chest?* Ahhh! I'll wager... of course! It is probably being sent to Ellis Island, that's routine; we must have thought it belonged to an immigrant. Miss Vognild. Our sincere apologies! I'll call the steward to bring you both a cup of tea. We'll have your chest back in no more than an hour, or even less if it hasn't left the ship yet."

Fifteen minutes later the baggage master brought her the chest. Marie, deeply relieved, tried to press a tip into the baggage master's hand.

"Oh, no madam, it really wouldn't be proper of me, but I thank you for the thought," he said. He got her baggage together and conducted Marie and Anna to a cab. They were on the way to Chicago where Anna was greeted by the big Vognild family, spent time at their Lake Marie summer cabin, saw the sights of Chicago, visited Evanston with Marie, and then headed back to Norway and Brekstad in time for the fall session of school.

A year later Marie went to a Sunday afternoon party at the home of her friend Molly Reffum. That was the day she met Gunnar.

Chapter 2

GUNNAR

Born on August 30, 1865, he was christened Gunnarius Emmanuel Abrahamsen for which he never really forgave his parents. From the time when he first became aware of his name he abhorred the pretentious Latinization of the very traditional Norwegian name Gunnar. As he grew older he saw the Emmanuel as a distasteful blow to the strong Lutheran faith of his mother. His last name he accepted with some reservations, branding it a relic of the popularity of biblical names and the subsequent patronymic period when the son of an early 18th century Norwegian Abraham would automatically take Abrahamsen as the family name. The "*sen*" ending was the equivalent of Abraham*son* in English or Swedish.

Granted, Abrahamsen indicated he was born into an established family. His father was becoming a successful furrier in the southwestern Norway seaport town of Stavanger, but far more important to Gunnar in his early youth, his father was also captain of the citizen guard and wore a saber and fine three-cornered hat when he paraded the guard down the street.

As a boy Gunnar had a thriving business. He had a large pigeon cote and sold baby pigeons and built and sold birdhouses to some of his companions. In the summer and fall he hurried down to the docks to meet the weekly boat from Hardanger with its cargo of fresh fruit and vegetables. He bought as much as he could load onto his little wagon and sell the produce house-to-house.

All this gave his parents hope that young Gunnar was really business-oriented and would eventually join the family firm, but they were overlooking the boy's current fascination with the sea. He spent many of his free hours watching ships being built and rigged. He knew that his mother's father had been a skipper who perished with his ship and crew in the big storm of 1828. But he understood they built ships better these days. He would not have to worry. He thought he would first be a cadet, then an officer in the navy. It might be some years, he regretted, because he was only 14 years old.

Just when he had made up his mind that he would go to sea despite any parental objections, the head teacher asked him to stay after school one day.

"Young man," old Tonnesen began, "Judge Hofgård has asked me to recommend a bright pupil to be a junior clerk in his office, that would mean spending a few hours after school every weekday afternoon. Of course you would be paid. It is a great opportunity. I have given the judge your name, and I hope you will accept the position."

Gunnar flushed, "You mean I would work for *Judge Hofgård himself?*"

"Well, not directly. He has clerks for whom you would work, but you would be in a fine position to decide whether you wanted to be a lawyer or a judge when you grow up. Can you go see Judge Hofgård after you have permission from your parents?"

The next afternoon Gunnar went to the little courthouse and was welcomed by the judge himself who thanked the boy for coming, asked him how his parents were and then introduced him to his head clerk. When the judge left the room, Ellingsen, the senior clerk, looked at Gunnar sternly.

"Boy," he said, "let us understand each other. You are to call me sir, you are to do as *I* say, and don't let me catch you loafing."

"Yes, sir," Gunnar replied. "But what am I supposed to be doing?"

The tasks were simple. He was to run to the post office when there were things to be mailed or mail to be fetched. He was to run other errands for the clerk. He was to copy documents Ellingsen gave him. "And you had better copy *accurately and neatly.* You can write, can't you?" Ellingsen asked.

"Yes sir," Gunnar said.

"Prove it," the clerk snapped, giving Gunnar a letter to copy.

Gunnar looked at the letter, then copied it with care. Proudly, he handed the copy to the clerk.

Ellingsen grunted disdainfully, "You call that writing? You will have to learn to do better than that." He walked away, leaving Gunnar sitting there.

In that same year Gunnar went each Saturday for six months to confirmation classes at the church. He was troubled by the burden he would be asked to undertake, forsaking the devil and all his works. According to the pastor almost all that mankind did was sinful. But Gunnar knew the judge smoked and even, when upset, he might curse softly. Gunnar's father also smoked, and he failed to go to church on many Sundays, and Gunnar had once seen him drink brandy.

The day came that Gunnar was to go before the minister and make his pledge to live a righteous, sin-free life. Without counseling first with his parents, Gunnar told Pastor Fjeldheim, "I don't think I can make the pledge to avoid sin, and I'm not even sure I believe all you have told us. So I am going to leave the class."

Pastor Fjeldheim was outraged. He warned Gunnar,

"You can be sure I will discuss this with your parents!"

Two days later Gunnar's father called him into his study. "I hear you are having trouble with Pastor Fjeldheim," he said, in as normal a conversational tone as he might use in observing that it was raining outside.

"Yes sir," Gunnar replied.

"You have to make up your own mind about these things," his father said, "but you should remember, failing to believe does not entitle you to live a careless, thoughtless life. You are still a human being. You can't escape your obligations." He puffed on his pipe for a few moments, then asked, "How is your work for the judge going?"

"Very well. But it has me thinking. I like what they do – the law. I think I want to go to the university in Kristiania and study law in a few years. Maybe I can become a lawyer or even a judge."

"Not a furrier?" his father asked.

"No sir. I don't have any desire for that. Besides, my brother Johan wants to be a furrier. There won't be place for me."

His father nodded, thought briefly, then said, "I am sure we can see that you get your education." He smiled and added, "It will be good to have a judge in the family."

Gunnar loved the outdoors and nearly paid with his life for one long hike that took him high up a mountainside. On his way down a he fell and barely escaped falling over a cliff. His leg was injured and he clung to a rock all night, then made his way down to the valley and hobbled home the next day.

In 1888 he took *artium* at Kongsgård school in Stavanger; this equivalent to a Bachelor of Arts entitled him to attend the university in Oslo as a graduate student for his law studies.

In those days there were no direct roads to the capital, no stagecoach and no train. When the time came for the long trip to Kristiania and the university, Gunner checked the cost of going by sea and decided to save money by walking. It took him several weeks up the old trail to Setesdal then across country through the Telemark area to Kristiania.

Student life in the capital of Norway opened a new world to Gunnar. He learned to tone down his Stavanger dialect and use what he called "city Norwegian." He also heard dialects from many parts of the country and became able to guess roughly where other students came from just through their speech patterns. He became a student of old Norse, the language of Iceland. He recognized the Danish influence on the Norwegian language and sensed the gradual return to pure Norwegian that would eventually become an irresistible tide as Norway returned to its root language. Above all he developed enormous interest in the United States and the democracy that was flourishing there. He started serious study of the English language and continued his study of law.

He listened with growing interest to student political discussions and began to participate in their shrill advocacy. There were two major issues. First, independence for Norway, an unwilling partner with and under Sweden as an aftermath of the Franco-German War. Second, socialism. Gunnar became a firebrand on both issues. He had carried the red socialist flag in a Mayday parade, and this was reported to his old patron, Judge Hofgård. The judge shook his head in disbelief and concern. Gunnar received a curt note from Hofgård: "You intended to become a lawyer and a judge?" he asked Gunnar. "Your conduct shocks me. I am afraid you have seriously compromised your future in the legal profession."

At the same time Gunnar was expecting an order to report for two years of military service, but in his passionate devotion to his native land he could not see serving under

Gunnar Abrahamsen —
Photographed in Stavanger
before leaving to America.

what would really be the Swedish flag. "Would they expect me to fire on patriotic Norwegians who were forced to fight for our national independence?" he asked in furious disbelief. He decided to go to the United States, as so many young Norwegians were doing in those days. He quit the university at the end of his third year, went home to say goodbye, and sought a new life across the ocean.

The journey was by sailing ship from Stavanger to England, then by English ship to New York. In 1889, at the age of 24, he came at last to Ellis Island, where he was asked his name. He replied with no hesitation, "Gunnar Lund, no middle name." He had finally achieved liberation from the hated Gunnarius Emmanuel. For his last name he had taken the name of a relative of his father's, he liked it. "Lund" in Norwegian is a grove of trees and his new name would remind him of nature at home.

He had heard of a city on the Pacific Coast called Seattle. Norwegians there had written letters that had been printed in *Stavanger Aftenblad*, the local newspaper. The letters were full of enthusiasm for the promise of this young city and the wonderful nature that was so similar to southern Norway. He came directly to Seattle by train and then, as his savings dwindled, hunted for the only kind of work he felt he could do – office work, preferably in a law office. But for a man who spoke English poorly with a heavy accent and was unable to write the language, he quickly learned an office job was impossible. Like so many educated immigrants, he had to start at the very bottom as a manual laborer.

His first job was shoveling gravel onto a flatcar for the Great Northern Railroad that was being built between Seattle and Mukilteo. In the evenings he ate, then fell into his bunk, aching in every muscle. The days were long, and the only thing that kept him going was his determination to keep up with the rest of the crew. His next job was laying track. Somewhat hardened now, he found this easier because there were quite a few periods of waiting and doing nothing, interrupted by bouts of body-numbing exertion.

He disciplined himself to spend his free time studying English, shedding his accent, and studying to take his test to become a citizen. He knew the work he was doing was not for him. He longed for books, for conversation that mattered. When he could stand it no longer, he drew his pay and returned to Seattle. He found no job there so he took work on the dock at Port Blakeley on Puget Sound loading lumber on schooners bound for San Francisco. On his second day he stopped to pull a big sliver from his hand. The supervisor shouted at him, "Greenhorn, get back to work - this is no place for sissies."

For a moment Gunnar fumbled for a retort, then shrugged his shoulders in disgust and walked off the job, He went back to Seattle where his hunt for work was again a failure. Gunnar learned that the eastern panic of 1893 and four year depression there was still being felt in the west.

Hearing that things might be better in Portland, he headed south in the middle of winter. All he could find was a temporary job as janitor in the Norwegian Lutheran Church. "As close to heaven as I may ever get," he later said.

In Portland the word was that things were better now in Chicago. He went there. He wound up in an egg-and-butter products business with Olaf Osland as a partner. For added income, he taught a church-sponsored evening class in English for Norwegian newcomers. Molly Reffum represented the church and attended each weekly meeting of the class. She took an active part explaining that she, too, needed to improve her English. After class one evening she invited him to a Sunday afternoon party at her home.

He dressed carefully for the party, wearing his new suit, a new tie and a stiff white collar not far different from the type he would wear all his life. Unsuccessfully he dampened his curly hair and attempted to brush it straight. Arriving at the Reffum home, he went forward to greet the hostess who was talking with a strikingly pretty young lady who spoke an unusual Norwegian. It blended the tonal structure of far northern Norway with what sounded like the farm dialect of the South Trondelag mountain district. However, she seemed to speak haltingly and often to grope for words as though she were from some other country.

Mrs. Reffum introduced the two and walked away. Her name was Marie Vognild. Gunnar, with his strong interest in the dialects of his native land, could not suppress what he feared might be unwelcome curiosity, "Perhaps I shouldn't ask, but are you from Norway?"

She smiled, "That's hard to say. In the last years I have lived in Chicago with my uncle and his family. He is from Oppdal and I just spent a year in Norway, much of it in Oppdal. I was born in far northern Vardø, but for years I usually spoke only Russian or German before coming to America."

He looked puzzled. "How did all that happen?" he asked and was suddenly fearful he might offend her.

"It's a very involved mystery," she replied. "We really wouldn't have time to go into it during a nice party like this. Shall we go have some coffee and cookies now?" She paused for a moment, then took his arm and led him to the dining room where, somehow, she was spirited away by another young woman but not before she could look back at Gunnar, smile, and say, "I really enjoyed meeting you, Mr. Lund."

"And I have very much enjoyed meeting you, Miss Vognild." He stood there a moment, wondering why his face suddenly felt so warm.

During the next days he waited impatiently for the meeting of the English class and an opportunity to ask about Miss Vognild. When Mrs. Reffum came to the class he drew her aside, thanking her again for the party. "I was very impressed with Miss Vognild," he began.

"Yes!" Mrs. Reffum interrupted, "Wasn't she beautifully dressed? She does it all herself. She is a very talented designer and dressmaker with quite a number of women working for her. She has wealthy customers all over Evanston."

Gunnar nodded, trying to suppress his dismay, his discouragement over the hopelessness of his situation. Here he was working in a very small business, fighting to make a living, and Miss Vognild who was a veritable princess was highly successful.

Mrs. Reffum was not one to be roundabout. "Would you like to meet her again?" she asked. "I could ask the two of you to some entertainment with us, if you wish."

Though he felt the situation was hopeless, he could not bring himself to say "no." "That would be very kind of you," he stammered.

So he met Marie again. She was lovely. She had about herself a calm self-assurance and a bearing he saw as regal. He liked the way she did her hair, rolled up almost like a crown. He liked her laugh, her vitality and dramatic gestures. She was unlike any other young woman he had ever met. He saw her as often as he could, and she seemed willing to

Marie Vognild — Chicago 1899.

spend time with him.

There were a number of reasons Marie was attracted to Gunnar. She was impressed with his conversational skills, his wide array of knowledge, his obvious ambition. He had told her of his continuing search to determine what his life work would be.

"But you have your work now in your business here in Chicago, don't you?" she reminded him.

He shook his head; "I have work, but not the work I want to do. I am making money, I am saving money, but that's not all there is to life. The Americans have a saying that fits me: 'Hitch your wagon to a star.' I believe in that, but I'm not ready yet. First, I am afraid I have to *make* my wagon. That's what I'm doing, learning business skills, learning to speak English like an American so I will not be seen as just another foreigner. And after I have that "wagon" built, then it will be time to find the star to which I can hitch my wagon."

She looked at him with a warm and admiring glance. "I like that about building your wagon. It seems to me you have really done that. And I know you will find the star you are looking for, Gunnar. You do have faith in yourself, don't you?"

"Of course I do. But," he glanced away, unable to continue with what he wanted to say because of a sudden feeling of shyness. Then he continued, choosing his words carefully, "But... Marie, I think I have to find that star, my

life's work, as quickly as possible… in order to, in order to…
" He stopped, then, looking down, started again, "Marie,
you have found your work. I haven't, can't you understand
that I must at least be doing as well as you if…." His voice
trailed off. He looked down, caught in a sudden wave of
hopeless inadequacy.

She smiled, looked fully at him and said softly, "I was
lucky Gunnar. It just happened to me without my even
looking for it. You'll find it because you *are* looking."

He nodded to show his gratitude.

In the next restless, desperate days, he realized he would
never find the kind of work he wanted in Chicago. There
might be a better chance in Seattle. He must stop seeing her.
He must concentrate on finding the work that would make
it possible to ask this fascinating, wonderful girl to marry
him. And when he did find that work, life could really begin.
But he could not resist the desire to see Norway one last
time, especially Stavanger and his people there. He sold his
interest in the butter-and-egg business to his partner and
left for Norway in early fall of 1899.

When he returned in the early spring he stopped in
Chicago to see Marie again before he continued to Seattle.
He asked, in the very formal way that Marie had come to
like, "May I write to you, Marie?"

"Of course you may, I hope you will… Please do!" She
took his hand. "You do not need to ask, I want you to write,
and I will write to you."

On the Sunday before he left Chicago he had been invited
for dinner at the home of Erik and Amalie Vognild, Marie's
aunt and uncle who had taken her into their family when
she first came to America. Gunnar was understandably
nervous. He knew it was highly important that he make a
good impression, but from the first moment he could feel

their approval.

"You have been to Seattle and are returning there," Erik said during dinner "I have heard from friends out there that it is a wonderful area. There are even a few people from Oppdal, I hear. Do you know any of them?"

"No, I am afraid I have never met anyone from your old home area," Gunnar replied.

Erik nodded, then said, "I can give Marie the names to put in a letter to you." Then he added with the hint of a smile, "if she writes."

Marie blushed. "Yes, uncle."

Gunnar turned to Mrs. Vognild, "But I can assure you I have met quite a few people from your area, Nordland and especially from Lofoten. Seattle is becoming a major center for fishermen from Norway."

She turned to her husband saying, "We must visit there some day, Erik. I would like very much to see the west." Years later, after her husband had died, Amalie Vognild made that trip to Seattle to visit Marie and her family.

Erik talked of his business and how difficult it had been to find competent people to work on customers' watches. For this reason he had opened Chicago's first watchmaker school, a most successful venture. The growth of immigrant population had led him to add a complete safe deposit vault to his jewelry business, and this, too, was highly successful. Apparently the Norwegian immigrants put more trust in a fellow Norwegian than in a bank.

Gunnar thought a moment, then said, "But Mr. Vognild, these things don't just happen. Most people complain of their problems. It must take a very shrewd business sense to see those problems as opportunities and take the appropriate actions and be successful at it."

"Let's just say that I have been unusually fortunate," Erik

laughed, and then added, "But tell me about your people and your home back in Norway."

Gunnar spoke of his father and mother, of Stavanger and how similar the climate and even the countryside was to Seattle. Then he added, "Seattle has unlimited opportunities. It has a magnificent deepwater harbor for trade with the Orient, an unlimited supply of pure drinking water, a great attraction for Norwegian immigrants in both fishing and agriculture. I see it as a city for the future." During dinner, Erik stood, raised his glass to Gunnar and said in the formal manner Norwegians so often use on such occasions, "I trust you will have every success in Seattle, a growing city needs young men of vision like you."

Marie saw him to the door where she whispered, "I knew they would like you."

They wrote to each other frequently. He told her of the beauty of Seattle with its forest-clad hills, Puget Sound, the Olympic Mountains to the west, and the glory of sunsets. He told her of the rain and of his slow progress in finding what he called his life's work. She, in turn, wrote him about their mutual friends in Chicago and asked him to tell her more about Seattle. Was there a Norwegian Lutheran Church? Were any of his friends married, and what were their wives like? He saw these questions as a good sign, and he answered them in detail.

Within a few months he landed a job at Frederick & Nelson, the major department store, and he told her in his letter that it was the Marshall Fields of Seattle. Now he was measuring for and installing shades, but the future looked good. The store was growing steadily and his progress was encouraging. He had received his first promotion.

Chapter 3

SEATTLE

Gunnar lived in a boarding house after returning to Seattle. His was a disciplined, austere life. He worked long hours to increase earnings and his savings. His only social life was an occasional evening out or weekend hours with Norwegian friends.

He wrote Marie regularly, telling her of the bustling Norwegian community with its many activities, the churches, the outings, and the weekly Norwegian language newspaper his friend Frank Oleson had started back in 1889. Gunnar was a subscriber at a dollar a year, and he sent several copies to Marie. He told her of his job and how he was progressing, and how he missed her.

Eventually, he was courageous enough to tell her what he really wanted to write about, his love for her. He counted the days waiting for a response. He could hardly hope to hear from her in less than two full weeks. On the sixteenth day, her letter came. She thanked him and told him that she loved him, too. Within the next few months she agreed to come west and marry him.

He sent her a ticket on the Northern Pacific Railroad that had recently built its line all the way to Seattle.

From the moment he met Marie at the train station, shyly

taking both her hands first, then holding her gently there on the busy platform, his life quickened. He had persuaded his friend Frank Oleson to act as his best man. Mrs. Oleson was the bride's attendant. The minister known as the marrying parson performed the simple ceremony. The date was September 6, 1900.

Marie had brought her red immigrant chest and several trunks filled with clothing. For the wedding she wore a stunning gown of pink dotted Swiss with a shawl collar. It was her creation, designed for this very special occasion. Gunnar was impressed. He wore a new suit. The Olesons drove them down to the pier and the newlyweds boarded the steamer for Victoria, the pleasant little city in British Columbia.

It was there that she gave him a handsome gold pocket watch as a wedding present from her aunt and uncle. On the face was the name of the maker, Erik Vognild. Gunnar's initials were engraved on the top. He would carry that watch through his entire life, the heavy gold chain looped through a vest buttonhole. When he needed to know the time, Gunnar pulled the watch out of his vest pocket and snapped open the top. He always did it with a great feeling of pleasure.

In Victoria, walking through the gardens, having tea, admiring the British wares in the shops and strolling along the waterfront, they found time to talk about their lives together and the kind of a house they would buy with the money Gunnar had saved. He told Marie that there were now tens of thousands of Norwegians in the Pacific Northwest, most of them in the Puget Sound region. New waves of them were now coming, especially from the fishing areas of Norway. There were Norwegian Lutheran churches, and talk of new organizations.

"And will I meet some of these new friends of yours?" she asked.

He smiled. "Some of them? All of them, and many more; I have had enough of being alone. From now on it is not I, Gunnar; it is the two of us, Marie and Gunnar," He took her hand. "It is a new world here, growing, lively, with a great future. I hope we can find happiness and success in being part of it."

He could hardly guess the part they both would play. He only knew that he now had Marie, that life was wonderfully exciting.

Marie shook her head when he suggested they start looking for a house to buy as soon as they returned to Seattle. "No, we must be practical about this," she said, "I don't know the city yet, let's just find a furnished flat to rent for the first six months or so."

By the end of the year they became homeowners. It was on Boylston Avenue just a short walk to the city center. That was where they had their first major quarrel.

When Gunnar came home one evening, Marie told him she had visited the city's best dressmaking establishment. "They do very good work and they have the best customers in Seattle," she reported. She paused, then continued, "They offered me a position as designer." She added quickly, "We could save much of what I would earn, and still afford to live in a better house than this."

Gunnar flared, "Marie, if you want to be a designer, you should go back to Evanston. It is the man's role to support the family. I will not tolerate having my wife work for a living."

"But Gunnar, be reasonable," she began.

He cut her off. "I don't want to hear about it again. I would be ashamed of myself if you had to work. It would be a disgrace I could not stand."

Marie held back her tears, she wondered if Gunnar saw her suggestion as criticism of his performance as the family wage earner. Unable to speak, she walked out of the room.

Later, he apologized. "Forgive me. I can't help the way I feel. I know you must be bored with nothing much to do. Please, Marie, find some interesting way to occupy your time — but let me fulfill my duties as the breadwinner."

She nodded. "I will try, but you must know that I was not being critical of you. I only wanted to help." She smiled. "I hope you don't really want me to go back to Evanston, Gunnar. My life is with you."

Struggling to find a way to mend the unpleasant breach he had caused, he said, softly, "Marie, there may be other times when I forget myself and speak harshly to you. I am inclined to be impetuous, to be overly critical. It is a hard habit to break. I will try because... because I never want to hurt you. Please believe that."

She accepted his apology, but she did not realize that in the years to come he would be unable to break the habit. When he opened a bill from Frederick & Nelson department store, from Helgesen Brothers delivery grocery, or from Wallin & Nordstrom the little one room local shoe store on Second Avenue which almost a century later would grow to the upscale nationally-known Nordstrom, he was provoked to verbal fireworks. "Woman," he cried, "Do you think I am made of money?"

Marie might try to explain her purchases, quietly saying, "But Gunnar, the children's shoes were worn out." Finding that tactic did not soften his outbursts, she more often took the rebuke in silence, unperturbed. She knew her husband. They knew each other. And the small things never seemed to matter. In the vernacular of a much later day, they had something going that was deep and permanent. And that became obvious, especially to their children.

That early quarrel made Gunnar evaluate his financial

progress. It was unsatisfactory, and he decided to cast around for better employment. He was aware that his knowledge of business was weak and that he had too little understanding of how a business should be managed. Explaining his need, he told Marie he planned to enroll in a night school class. She was enthusiastic about the idea and encouraged him to do it. One night each week he attended a class in business basics, but that also meant he had to study a number of hours each week in the evenings.

During these classes he sat next to Karl Johnson, a young man of Swedish parentage who was having trouble with his homework and needed help. Gunnar gave it, finding he was the real learner through having to help another.

As the class drew toward its end, the students were asked to report their solutions to a typical set of business problems, what later would be known as the popular case history approach to business. Gunnar studied the given details and at once saw a similarity with the Vognild Jewelry situation back in Chicago. In his verbal report he pointed out the apparent problems and applied what he called the "conversion principal" – the turning of problems into opportunities – and showed how several of the firm's problems could be transformed into new sources of revenue or greater efficiency of operation with reduced costs.

The instructor was visibly impressed and hearty in his congratulations. As Gunnar took his seat, Karl thumped him on the shoulder.

After one of the classes they were walking together when Karl said, "Gunnar, you have taught me that it is not true that a Norwegian is a Swede with his brains knocked out. You really seem to understand what the teacher is trying to give us."

Gunnar laughed. "I heard that saying the other way

around, but your way may be right." They parted and Gunnar went home to Marie and another week of homework.

After the next session, Karl asked Gunnar to be his guest for a nightcap of coffee. When they were seated, Karl asked, "Are you happy with your present work?"

"Not really," Gunnar answered, "I don't seem to be getting anywhere – that's why I'm in the class."

"I told my dad about you and he would like to see you." Karl said, "Dad owns a dairy and he feels that with your butter-and-egg experience in Chicago there might be a similar opportunity for you here."

Three weeks later Gunnar had his own business. He purchased his butter from Karl's father, who had also helped him find a wholesale source for eggs. It was work he knew and enjoyed. Gunnar's income grew. All deliveries were made by horse-drawn wagon. At the start, Gunnar did his own solicitation house-to-house and performed his own delivery service. Within a few months he saw the good sense of hiring a driver-salesman and that proved so successful that soon he had two driver-salesmen and he spent all his time managing the business and handling tasks of the office and small warehouse.

One of Gunnar's good Norwegian friends was Olaf Toft, a fellow immigrant who was spending his free time in trying to start a Sons of Norway lodge. He approached Gunnar one day and asked if he would help promote the idea. Gunnar was enthusiastic and began to talk about it with his growing circle of Norwegian friends.

The lodge was to be called Leif Erikson Lodge #1, the beginning of what they hoped to see as a West Coast group of lodges. On April 26, 1903, the lodge was founded with Toft as president and Gunnar as vice-president. Later he was to be elected president of the lodge and then president of the Grand Lodge. Eventually it merged with the larger Midwest Sons of Norway to become District #2, and Gunnar was a major proponent of the merger. The lodge brought local Norwegian men together for monthly meetings and sponsored many popular activities.

Almost immediately, the wives of the Sons of Norway members started talking about the idea of a lodge for women to be called the Daughters of Norway. Marie was to become a charter member and would serve as president and later as Grand Lodge president. Gunnar and Marie were broadening their circle of friends in the west's Norwegian-America, and their acquaintances and influence were to expand even more dramatically during the years ahead.

In 1903, Marie gave birth to their first child. It was on December 13 and they named him after Marie's father, Johannes, using the more common Anglicized version of John with Vognild as his middle name. Gunnar and Marie began to think of a larger house and they found it on the very steep hill close to the end of Belmont Avenue North. They had a view of Lake Union, it was close enough to town for Gunnar to walk to and from his little company. They had more room than they really needed and in the heavy expenses that came in 1905, Gunnar finally gave in to Marie's pleading and allowed her to take in two women teachers as boarders. As she said to her closest friends, "It's my way of helping Gunnar in this major step he is taking. We really need the extra income right now."

In 1904 Gunnar had a visit from Karl Johnson's father, the owner of the small dairy through which he purchased his supply of butter. Johnson was impressed with the growth of Gunnar's firm. He asked a number of questions about how the business operated then said, "Gunnar, let me make you a proposition. I am suggesting that I buy your business and merge it with mine. I will also pay you for whatever time it takes you to train my boy Karl to manage the delivery business."

Gunner was offered a very favorable price and accepted immediately. When he came home to tell Marie, she asked, "But Gunnar, now what will you do?"

"It's back to shades, but not just measuring," he replied. "When I worked for the department store we had a competitor, Pacific Window Shade Company. They know me and have been interested in employing me. I talked to them today. They want me for more than measuring and selling window shades; they want me to manage their outside department. I would only do that until I can find something better."

She looked at him, feeling he might be holding something back. "Something better? What do you mean?"

"Marie," he paused, "I really don't know. I only know that, up to now, I haven't found work that satisfies me. I see my friends having *careers*, as engineers, as politicians, as doctors, as lawyers like Frank Oleson. And I can't seem to find out who I am or what I am good for."

"Gunnar," she said quietly, "I know what you are, a dear, good, honest, hard working man. Isn't that enough?"

His answer came quickly, "You know it isn't. Not for you, not for me."

He went to work for Pacific Window Shade, hiring, training and managing the men who drove buggies around the growing city, selling shades, measuring for them, and delivering and installing them. Because he worked long hours and knew the business, he did well, but for him it was only a stopgap and he kept looking for something better. The payment for his butter-and-egg business went into his savings account. It was there for some future opportunity, perhaps to buy a business. He was not sure.

In his worst moments Gunnar thought of himself as a man without a trade, a drifter, a failure. In his mind he went back over his life. He had studied law and expected the law would be his career, but he had taken a youthful politically wrong turn and left Norway because of it. Coming to Seattle and been unable to find a suitable position, so he loaded lumber, shoveled gravel onto freight cars, helped lay railroad track, left for Portland looking for any work he could find, and wound up shoveling coal into a church furnace. He had gone to Chicago, built a small business there, sold it and taken a trip home to Norway. He had come back to Seattle, the city he loved, and though he had made progress and he was saving money, he was not doing what he wanted to do. The worst of it was that he had not even decided what it was that he wanted to do.

What was to become of him? Married to this wonderful woman who before she was of age had found her career and been a great success, and then left it to marry him! At the age of 40 he was still drifting, with nothing achieved. True, he would be forty years old in just two months on the thirtieth of August.

"I was wrong to sell the butter-and-egg business," he told himself, "Johnson paid me well which proves he realized its value. It appears now I did not share his view and quickly took the money and ran. I can't go on jumping from one thing to another. I know the shade business but starting my own company would hardly be the fair thing. Might there be a chance of buying my way into a partnership? Or is the window shade business what I want to be doing the rest of my life?"

These were difficult, frustrating months for Gunnar. He paid more attention to the daily newspaper, looking for hints that might point him to a worthwhile career. What businesses were growing? Where were the opportunities? He found no easy answers. He would take a pad of foolscap and list his capabilities, trying to find anything that would point to an attractive future career.

At the monthly Sons of Norway meetings he would do his utmost to be positive and outgoing, hoping someone who had a business opening would notice him and pull him aside. He was always the first to volunteer when members were recruited to go to another city to help form a lodge. Who knows, there might be opportunity there for him – a better job, a chance to go up.

He tried to hide his growing desperation from Marie, but she knew his anguish and the cause. Marie thought of herself in her own phrase as a "hopeful fatalist" – one who knew that in the darkest moment fate would intervene and all would be well. In all the years to come she never lost that faith. Her optimism was boundless, and she tried to impart that to Gunnar. "You *must*," she insisted, "You *must* have faith, Keep looking, keep thinking positive thoughts. It *will* come for you. I know it will."

He would smile, and sadly shake his head. "Yes Marie, I know. But something I am doing is wrong. Good things just aren't coming for me. I just can't seem to find them."

Chapter 4

THE STAR

Nineteen hundred five was a big year for Norway. The June news from the capital city of Kristiania was of enormous interest to Norwegian immigrants. The government had dissolved its union with Sweden but the Swedish parliament refused to accept that action. Troops were mobilized in both countries but negotiations continued and agreement was finally reached. Norway was again an independent country with a new king: Prince Charles of Denmark was called to serve as King Haakon VII.

Norwegians at home were not the only ones reveling in the joys of nationalism and independence. In Seattle, Norwegian-Americans were equally thrilled. They celebrated the event. There was speechmaking and applause.

One Seattle Norwegian-American had reasons to celebrate both for Norway and for himself personally. Looking back, he saw that 1905 had completely changed his life. He had found the mission he knew he needed. This mission gave him a strong sense of purpose and progress, but in that first sink-or-swim year, while he could cheer the developments in Norway, he could hardly celebrate his own situation. He was fighting for economic survival and the survival of what he and many others would felt was a valuable and even essential institution.

Gunnar's personal drama of 1905 began in this way. Frank Oleson, Gunnar's best man at his wedding, had completed his law training and had begun a career that would make him a leading Norwegian-born attorney in the state. He called Gunnar one day to ask if he could meet him at his law offices. The meeting should be as soon as possible, the next day if Gunnar could be free. It was urgent.

"Is anything wrong?" Gunnar asked.

"No, no." Frank replied, "but it *is* important! Can you make it at ten tomorrow morning?"

Gunnar arrived at ten. Frank seated him and after an exchange of greetings, asked, "How are you doing in the shade business? Is it everything you've hoped for?"

Gunnar's reply was not enthusiastic; "I'm not in it for the fun of it, Frank. It's a stopgap for me until I find something I want to do for the rest of my life."

Frank smiled. "Gunnar, your luck has turned. I called you because there's something available to you that can be the life work you have been searching for, where you can really make a contribution.

Gunnar looked at him quizzically. "And what in the world could that be? Certainly not the law, that's in the past for me."

"No, not the law, *journalism*."

"The little Norwegian language newspaper? But Frank, that's ridiculous, I don't know anything about journalism. No, Frank, that can't be for me. Besides, everyone knows it's a white elephant. Do you still own an interest in the paper?"

"Just a minority interest. But I gave it birth and I want it to survive. Let me tell you what the situation is."

"Frank, I am not interested. I couldn't ever consider it."

Frank held up his hand. "Gunnar, hold your horses. At

least let me tell you about it."

"Go on if you must, but my answer will still be 'no'," Gunnar objected.

Frank continued, "When I decided to study law, I hired an editor to run the paper. For a while that worked very well, but then it drifted from one person to another. In disgust I finally sold it to a corporation that published Norwegian and Swedish papers, but that didn't work out either. So I pumped some money into it and got some other investors which enabled me to try to make it go with a new editor. Now we are holding the bag. The last editor has taken off. The only reason the paper came out last week is that I spent some long evening hours acting as editor on top of my law work.

"Now let me tell you the truth. We do not have many paid subscribers, but the potential is excellent here in the west, in California, Oregon and Washington, plus British Columbia and Alaska. Think how important such a weekly newspaper can be to your friends and mine, multiplied many times over. It tells them what is happening back home in the Norway they can never forget. It keeps them abreast of what is happening in their churches and their organizations here. It helps them become successful here in America, and yes, to be better Americans.

"Gunnar, this little newspaper has a great future with the right man as its owner and editor, and I am taking your time because I know you are the man who can give it what it needs."

Gunnar laughed. "Frank, you are wasting your time in law, you should become a salesman. But you are not a magician. How in the world can you change me into an editor? This whole idea is ridiculous."

"Listen carefully now, Gunnar. You can write. I know that. I've seen what you did helping develop the by-laws and the appeal for Leif Erikson lodge. You know business. Most of all, you know Norway and Norwegians." Then, his impatience showing, "Really think about the opportunity you have, not only to be an editor and publisher and owner, but to help our people – and to make for yourself a fine, profitable career."

He saw that Gunnar was not weakening. "Gunnar, understand me. Listen to me. I'm not doing this just to get rid of the paper. I'm doing this because I have given it a lot of thought. I have been searching for the man who has the native talent and knowledge of business to make the paper succeed. You are the very man this opportunity can mean something to. It can change your life and give you the career you deserve. Your name keeps coming up. You need it and it needs you. It's that simple. All three of us partners agree that you are the man."

Frank stopped, exasperated by Gunnar's obvious lack of interest. On an impulse, he changed course. "Then do something just for friendship's sake. Ask Marie what *she* thinks. There isn't much time. You can't think this over for the next six months. The major owner is Arne Solberg and he is handling the sale, He's the man you have to see, and he is trying to hold things together at the *Washington Posten* office. Call him or go see him.

Frank rose from his chair and put out his hand, "Will you promise to talk with Marie about this?"

Gunnar's handshake was anything but his normal firm grip. He nodded his head, but as he left the room he was shaking his head in disbelief. Frank's confidence in him, his own lack of fitness for the position, only one word came to his mind *gal* the Norwegian word that means "crazy." It applied both to Frank and the idea that he, Gunnar, could ever become an editor.

Incredulous, he returned to his office and the business of selling shades. Arriving home at the close of that day he exchanged his suit coat for an old threadbare one – a custom that became a habit. When he sat down to the dinner Marie had prepared he found he could not eat.

"Marie," he said, "there is something I have promised Frank Oleson to discuss with you." And he told her of the meeting with Frank.

She sat spellbound, waiting for every word. "Gunnar!" she exclaimed, "This is what you have been looking for!"

"I – looking for?"

"Of course. Remember? Back in Chicago when I first knew you, you were talking about hitching your wagon to a star. You said you didn't have a star and what was worse, you didn't even have a wagon yet. By wagon you meant business skills, knowledge, abilities. You have built that wagon, and I'm proud of you. You are a good business manager. You speak and write very well. I have heard you speak; I have seen what you write. Now you can hitch your wagon to that star you wanted to find – your real life's work. It wasn't in selling butter and eggs. You have said many time that it isn't in measuring and selling window shades. It's in being an editor, building *Washington Posten*, being of service not only to Norway and Norwegian-Americans, but to these wonderful United States as well. Gunnar, think what it can mean – for both of us!"

"I don't know," he said. "I feel inadequate. I'm not a journalist. I don't know anything about running a newspaper. And think of the risk! Think of the possibility of failure! Nobody has made it work up to now. The paper has probably lost money since the day it started. I know it has had at least six owners, and two of them were corporations, good business firms that couldn't make it. What indication is there that I could be successful?"

Marie had a ready answer, "The butter-and-egg business you built in Chicago and also here, and what you are doing at the shade company. Gunnar, you are a successful businessman!" She struggled to find a way to convince him and give him confidence. After a moment she said, quietly, "Think of what you could do to make it work, to make it successful, to turn it into a profitable business. You told me about your answer on the case history in the business class. You did the same thing in your butter-and-egg business. Please think of the problems in making the paper successful, and how you can turn them into opportunities. Do that right now."

He sighed. "Well, first it has too few subscribers. Second, it is losing money – though that may be because they have their own printing plant with all the typesetters and other workers. Maybe they ought to buy their printing from a large print shop. And third, there have been far too many changes of ownership and editorship. People don't know what to expect next. I imagine they feel it will fail."

She knew her husband. He might not immediately be able to find a way to convert those problems into opportunities, to use the "conversion principle" he had developed for his business class, but his mind would work at it and he would, impatiently, dig for the facts he needed to find answers. In finding them, he would overcome his concerns and begin to realize what an opportunity this was.

She took his hand, "Think of those problems, Gunnar, and you will find answers. I know you will."

"But Marie," he objected. "We don't have the funds. It would be impossible to buy the paper as Frank suggests."

"We *do* have enough to make a down payment. The money you got for your butter-and-egg business is in the bank for just this kind of an opportunity," she replied. "But

go ahead, think about how you would solve the problems."
She paused, then her voice changing, she said with great
conviction, "Gunnar, this is the star you have been looking
for, and I remind you again, you now have the wagon to
hitch to it. I am so proud of all you have learned and all you
can do. I want you to know something. I beg you to do it: I
have every faith that you will be wonderfully successful."

He looked at her, smiled, and said, "You have far too
much confidence in me. More than I have in myself. But...
maybe I should do as you say. Well, anyway, let me think
about it."

He did not sleep much that night nor did she. Over
morning coffee she looked at him, raising her eyebrows to
ask the question that was in her mind.

He sighed. "I will talk to Arne Solberg . It might be the
thing to do. Might be, I remind you. It still seems a great, a
dangerous gamble."

She kissed his forehead as he left for work. From the
shade company he called Solberg and set up an appointment
at the newspaper office in the old Metropolitan Building.

Solberg and Gunnar settled down in chairs in the
newspaper office which Gunnar thought was disgracefully
messy. There were piles of old newspapers on a table, two
cluttered roll top desks and several dilapidated chairs. The
scene was less than impressive.

Solberg was not a man to waste words. He immediately
announced the price, which was far, more than Gunnar was
prepared to pay. When he asked about terms, Solberg replied
one third would be required in down payments, the balance
in two installments payable every six months.

Gunnar was dismayed. "I am afraid it is more than I
should obligate myself to. May I think this over for a few
days?"

Solberg agreed. They shook hands and Gunnar left. That night he told Marie of his meeting and his plan to go back to see if he could negotiate a lower price and better terms. However, when he called Solberg the next afternoon, he was told that a young man, Martin Apland, had agreed to the terms and was taking immediate possession.

Gunnar thanked Soldberg and hung up the phone. Numb with disappointment and self-recrimination, he went out to his buggy, took the reins and sat there for a few moments. He felt he had missed the chance of his lifetime. He dreaded telling Marie but knew he had to face it. As he drove to his office he began thinking of what he could have done to bring *Washington Posten* into profitability. There were no shortcuts, he knew. Perhaps he could trim staff. Perhaps he could increase the subscription price. No, not until he had improved the paper. How long would that take? What could he do in the short term and what had to be done in the long term? He shook his head, knowing that it was too late. He had missed the chance. He had lost the star to which he could hitch his wagon. He recognized in anguish that he had lost the opportunity he had searched for such a long time.

At home, Marie was equally disappointed, though she tried to hide it. Finally she asked, "Gunnar, what are you going to do now?"

"It's queer, Marie. But I think that brooding over this misstep has to stop. I have to start looking, actively, for my real life's work. Suddenly it appears all the money in the world will not make it worthwhile to continue in the window shade business. But I can't walk away from it, we need the income…"

Marie interrupted him, "No, Gunnar, we have that money in the bank. Quit your job and spend time looking, now!"

Gunnar laughed. "You know me better than that. I intend

to keep on doing what I'm doing, but I shall spend every possible hour looking for my real work."

On Friday, July 21 when Gunnar came home from his work, he went immediately to his reading chair where Marie always put his mail for the day. He picked up the copy of *Washington Posten* and promptly opened it to page 4. There, at the top of the left-hand column he saw what he expected, "Martin Apland, Editor." He laid the paper down, shrugged his shoulders to get rid of the despair he felt, and went to look for Marie.

Months passed. No matter how much Gunnar looked, he found nothing of real interest. In the first week of November Marie left for Chicago with their young son John. She had missed her Uncle Erik Vognild's funeral, but she wanted to spend time with her aunt and the family.

While she was gone, Arne Solberg called. Young Apland had given up, he was unable to make his next payment on *Washington Posten*. Was Gunnar still interested? Gunnar immediately asked for an appointment for the next day and insisted on getting a first-refusal assurance. He wanted to be positive Solberg would not sell to anyone else in the meantime. From the Western Union office he sent a wire to Marie asking her opinion. The next morning the answering telegram was delivered. He opened it quickly and was relieved by its message:

"DON'T WAIT BUY IT IMMEDIATELY AT ANY PRICE LOVE MARIE."

He met Solberg at the *Washington Posten* office.

"Mr. Solberg," he said. "I can understand you are disappointed. It is my opinion that Apland failed because you set your price too high. There is no way he – or anyone – could take enough profit out of this paper to meet such steep payments. I understand that in its first sixteen years the paper has now had seven or eight owners. The paper is too run down. It has had too many failures of ownership." He paused.

Solberg nodded.

"Washington Posten," Gunnar continued, "is now a piece of very badly shopworn merchandise. If you want to sell it to me, or to anyone, you will have to set a more realistic price with longer terms. Unless you do, you will guarantee the paper's next failure."

Solberg was silent for a few moments. "How much are you prepared to pay?" he asked.

"First, let me see the books, I want to know where the business stands," Gunnar countered.

"It's not a pretty picture," Solberg stated, "The business owes a little in shop wages, and there is very little money in the bank, not enough to meet the obligations." He took the worn general ledger from a desk drawer and gave it to Gunnar.

Gunnar examined it slowly and asked a few questions. Then he took a piece of paper out of his breast pocket, looked for a moment at the price and terms he was willing to accept, pulled out a signed check, and gave it and the paper to Solberg.

Solberg studied the paper and the check. There was a long pause before he looked directly at Gunnar. "Frank Oleson tells me you are a man of honor and determination and that you have the ability to succeed. I guess that is what we need. The price you suggest is low, the terms are more lenient than I'd like, but as Frank says, we are not in a position to 'dicker.' We need to get the paper into the hands of a person who can succeed and meet his commitment to us."

As he listened, Gunnar could feel his spirits rise. Then he said, "I do not intend to fail, Mr. Solberg."

Solberg put out his hand, "I will accept, providing you

can take charge immediately."

"No, that is hardly possible. I must give my employer the customary two weeks' notice. I am not in the habit of turning my back on obligations." Gunnar waited.

Solberg showed his disappointment. He looked down, thought a moment, then said, "If Frank can help us out, I guess we have a deal. Let me call him." When Frank answered, Solberg explained that Gunnar was asking for a two-week delay before starting. "Can you help out in the meantime, Frank?"

Gunnar could not overhear Frank's reply, but he saw Solberg smile and say, "Fine. We'll go ahead, then." He hung up the phone. "Frank is delighted to hear that you are buying the paper. He will work here evenings, and will welcome your help. This might be your best opportunity to find out what the work is like."

Gunnar waited, suddenly feeling the precariousness of his situation. He had offered to take responsibility for this "white elephant" as several of his friends had called it. The check he had written amounted to the greater part of the family's savings. It left very little for operating capital. Now there was no turning back. Then he chuckled at his own sense of concern.

Gunnar drove to his office at the shade company. Apologizing for leaving on such short notice, he explained why he was leaving and expressed his hope that they might find and hire a replacement quickly so he would have the opportunity to train him and introduce him to the best customers on his list. Before he left, he telephoned Frank Oleson and arranged to meet him at the newspaper office at six that evening. On his way he sent a wire to Marie:

CONGRATULATIONS YOU NOW WIFE OF WASHINGTON POSTEN PUBLISHER LOVE GUNNAR

There was no one in the one-room editorial office when Gunnar arrived, but he could hear printers still at work in the shop at the rear. Soon Frank came and took him on a tour of the print shop where he met the foreman, Julius Sunde, a likeable fellow and obviously one respected by his little crew of printers.

Back in the editorial office, Gunnar turned to his old friend, "Frank, I want you to know that it is with fear and trembling that I am doing this. Tell me where I start. How do I get my first issue out? I'm not worried about the business details, I think I can learn them on my own. What I need to know is what do I do, as editor, to get the paper written and printed."

"Well," Frank started, "First, you are in luck. This is Wednesday evening and all the copy is in for the week's issue. The paper must be printed first thing tomorrow, Thursday morning, so the printers can take it to the post offices and a few general newsstands where it is sold. The only thing we must do tonight is read, correct and approve the page proofs. Sunde is just about to pull the proofs and bring them in, I imagine. When he does, I'll go over them with you. So what we should do now is talk about next week's paper and how we get and edit the news to fill it."

Gunnar nodded, "That's my first question, how do we get it, where does it come from?"

Frank took a copy of the previous week's paper. As he spoke he pointed at examples of the various types of news. "Most of it comes to you in the mail or in person, from the ministers about their churches, from the Norwegian organizations, and from exchange papers; we don't get enough of them from Norway, but we do get them from many of the Norwegian-American weekly press. You haven't time to read them carefully, but you must scan them for any items you can clip and paste or rewrite. Some stories you must get on your own, either by phone or by personal interview. Do you know how to prepare copy for the printer?"

Gunnar shook his head. Frank took a piece of newsprint copy paper, half the size of ordinary three-ring binder paper, roughed in a headline and drew lines to represent text. "This is the convenient size for the printer. Use this copy of the newspaper to give you an idea of how many letters your headline can be, and this is how you count them." He pointed out the letters "m" and "w" counted as one and a half letters, while an "i" and "l" each counted as half a letter.

Headline writing would be no major chore for Gunnar. The headlines were simply one line of standard 8-point type in boldface capitals. Gunnar looked at his notes, then looked up at Frank, "But how does the shop know what story goes where? Does Sunde determine that?"

Frank answered, "No, not entirely. You know each week what articles you have sent in to the printers. A lot of the placement is automatic. Routine Seattle news goes to page 8 and can carry over to page 4. Coast city news goes to page 3, Norway news usually to page 2, and the weekly serial to page 5 or 7. Everything has its place – except! And the exception is news from anywhere, Norway or San Diego or Seattle, so big that it deserves to go on the first page. You do that juggling in your head during the week and you tell Sunde anything that can't be left to his judgement, such as the stories that go to page one, or other stories that should have special placement.

"Now, Gunnar," Frank continued, "Let me tell you how we make sure everything turns out right. You will write copy – that's what we call the articles that are to run in the paper. You will take the copy into the shop. The printers will set it into type, one letter at a time, including the headlines, and when they have a full galley – that's a little shorter than a column - they will pull galley proofs. These will come to you to be read and corrected and sent back with any corrections to the shop.

"Now comes what American editors call 'putting the paper to bed.' First we check the shop to make sure all the corrections have been made from the galley proofs we sent back to them. Then we show Sunde what we want on the front page, which stories go where. We help him in any problems or questions he may have on the layout of the other pages. The advertising salesman usually takes care of placement of the ads.

"Finally we have Sunde make page proofs of the individual pages and we check each of them as we will do any minute now. Generally the shop foreman knows what should go where. We just want to make sure he has made the right decisions. We check all the little details, such as when an article is continued from page one to another page. Is there the proper 'continued' line and is the continuation on the right page with a 'continued from' line and the appropriate new heading. When we are satisfied, we give the word to start printing."

They were interrupted by Sunde who came in with proofs from the eight pages. Frank and Gunnar went through the proofs rapidly, with Frank guiding Gunnar in making corrections.

When they had finished they carried the proofs out to the shop. Sunde looked them over, nodded his understanding and gave the proofs to one of the printers for the few changes that had to be made.

Gunnar was delighted with what he later called "Frank's quick class in journalism for innocent beginners." Frank's detailed presentation was put to a stop by their hunger. They went out for a quick dinner. Instruction continued through the meal. At eleven they shook hands and left the office.

That night Gunnar had trouble getting to sleep. He thought of many questions that he had not asked Frank. When he finally fell asleep, he was disturbed by a vivid nightmare: there was not enough news to fill the paper and he could plainly hear Sunde and the other printers shouting for more copy.

In the morning he dressed hurriedly, had a quick breakfast and walked the long trip to the shade company office. It was seven thirty when he arrived at work. To the last day of work in his life, his arrival time never varied.

Before six each evening he was back at the newspaper office for more instruction from Frank plus actual work in writing or editing stories, writing headlines, and correcting galley proofs. By the beginning of the second week, with Frank's helpful coaching, he was developing familiarity and increasing comfort with the work routine. On one of the last evenings he told Frank, "I think you have helped me get over my 'fear and trembling.' Now it's just a matter of learning to do things well. So what are your final instructions?"

Frank handed him a copy of the previous week's paper, "Turn to the top of the left hand column of page four." Gunnar did as he was told. Frank continued, pointing, "This is the masthead. From now on you are the publisher and editor. Your name should go here, right at the top of this first column under the name and address of the newspaper. Take your scissors and cut out the masthead. Cut out the old names, Paste the masthead on a piece of copy paper and pencil in what you want it to say from now on."

Gunnar followed Frank's instructions but stopped to think a moment before he wrote 'Gunnar Lund, Publisher.'

Gunnar Lund, Editor and Publisher of the Washington Posten — Seattle 1905.

"Not editor and publisher?" Frank asked.

Gunnar smiled. "Maybe I'll add 'editor' when and if I'm no longer worried about how questionable my editing is."

"Apland's business manager left with him," Frank began, "So you may need to find yourself a new person to handle billing for circulation and advertising and collections and the business books. Any ideas about whom you might hire?"

"Nobody," Gunnar replied. "I'll save money by handling that myself."

Frank nodded in agreement and they took the copy for the masthead in to Sunde, the shop foreman. Sunde looked at it a moment and smiled. He wiped his hands on his printer's apron and then held out his hand to Gunnar, "Let me be the first to congratulate you. I wish you well. This week's paper will carry the date of November 17, 1905. It is a great day for *Washington Posten*."

On this, Frank's last evening of coaching, they left early for dinner. As they were eating, Gunnar remarked, "Frank, if this weren't a crowded restaurant I would stand and make a formal speech of thanks. How can I ever repay you for all you have done?"

Frank did not hesitate with his response. "I'll get plenty of payment with every copy of *Washington Posten* I read in the many, many years to come. Gunnar, you once told me what you were looking for in life. Do you agree that you

61

have found it?"

Gunnar nodded. "I think maybe I have, thanks to you." He thought a moment, then added "And thanks to Marie."

Later, Gunnar would say that it took a long, hard year before he felt he was making any real progress. He made his payment at the end of the year. By the end of the second year he could report that he now owned *Washington Posten* free and clear.

But Marie would never forget the first few months. At night, and it could be late, Gunnar would come home with a large envelope full of work to do during the evening. He worked every Saturday and many Sundays. She was concerned over his health, yet he seemed to be thriving. "Gunnar," she said, "You must not work such long hours. You must have more time to relax and rest."

He nodded his head but kept working.

Chapter 5

FIRST YEARS

While Gunnar was in the process of finding his life work,
learning how to be a successful editor and fighting to turn
his "white elephant" *Washington Posten* around, there were
a number of important developments in the Lund family.
John had been born in 1903. Helga was born in 1906. In 1908
Marie was ill. Dr. Adolf Loe spoke of "incipient tuberculosis"
and recommended outdoor living. The family moved to Alki
Point, just beyond the end of the streetcar line and a full
hour from downtown Seattle. In those days the Alki district
held only a few farms and but few houses. Marie took it
very easy. One day she, John and Helga went for a walk up
through the nearby pasture toward the woods. Suddenly she
stopped and motioned for the children to be quiet. Staring
at them was what she called a wildcat, its tail twitching.
"Children," she whispered, "Sing with me!" She began
singing and they sang with her:

What a friend we have in Jesus
All our sins and griefs to bear.
What a privilege to carry
Everything to Him in prayer . . .

The cougar slunk away. That was the end of their walks
up through the farmer's pasture. When Marie was much

improved the family moved back to their house on Belmont Avenue North.

***

Early in 1991 when Helga and Roald were planning to write the history of their parents and the paper, Roald called the office of the successor newspaper, Western Viking, to ask permission to review the old *Washington Posten* bound files. He was disappointed to learn they had all been sent to Minneapolis where they were being converted to microfiche. The film was not expected back for a year or more. That was one more reason, or excuse, for not writing the story at that time.

In 1999 when the embers of resolution once again began to glow, Roald called *Western Viking* and was told the microfiche had been deposited at the Suzzalo Graduate Library of the University of Washington in Seattle. He called there, assuming that he would have to go to that location to read the microfiche reels, but was advised he could request them through his local library and they would be sent to the Tigard library by inter-library transfer at a nominal cost.

Three weeks after his request the Tigard Library called to report the first batch of reels had arrived, covering the years from 1904 to 1918. Thus began the adventure of seeing the past life of the Norwegian-American colonies on the West Coast through the files of *WashingtonPosten*.

Each reel held two years of the weekly paper. Making a printed copy was simple and cost only 10 cents — simple, providing the original document was crisp and clean. Unfortunately, newsprint contains its own destructive acids, and the newspaper had turned yellowish and in some cases almost black. Working with files that were 50 to 90 years old before being microfilmed became an eye-wearying task for an 87-year-old reader. In a few cases the film pages were so dark and blurred they were very difficult to read and did not allow a legible copy to be printed.

The oldest microfiche files presented a daunting problem. Even so, it was worth the effort since a clear picture emerged of how Gunnar was changing *Washington Posten*, and especially, how *Washington Posten* was changing Gunnar. They also indicated how the Norwegian-American communities in Seattle and along the West Coast were growing and what key events occurred during Gunnar's years as editor and publisher.

***

The featured story on page one of Gunnar's second issue, November 24, 1905 called for a big type headline. There was rejoicing in Norway. Prince Charles of Denmark had been elected king of Norway and would be crowned as King Haakon VII in the historic eight hundred-year-old Nidaros Cathedral at Trondheim in June of 1906. There was a large picture of King Haakon and Queen Maud.

The only sign that something had changed at *Washington Posten* was in the masthead at the top of page four, column one, where a new name appeared: Gunnar Lund, Publisher. He did not list himself as editor because he felt it might appear presumptuous. He let that wait until he was sure of himself in the editor role. He did not list himself as business manager because that would indcate another change. His decision not to hire a business manager cut one cost item out of the payroll. He knew if he could at least maintain the same income the paper would be making money, especially if he could increase the number of subscribers. Later he would hire a solicitor, but for the present he would make sure he was personally present at all Norwegian gatherings. He decided the best way to get more subscribers would

65

simply be to ask people to subscribe.

Gunnar's name had been in *Washington Posten* a number of times since he became president of the Seattle lodge of Sons of Norway the previous year. Those mentions included his presiding over meetings and appearing at programs such as the big Seventeenth of May program when he had been the first speaker, welcoming the attendees. He was now fairly well known among Norwegian-Americans in the Seattle area. That, he knew, would be of some help to him.

He debated whether to include in his first issue a major article or editorial about his plans for the paper. He scaled that down in his mind to a brief story, but finally he decided it would be safer and more appropriate to use his name as publisher in the masthead as the only acknowledgement there had been any change.

In explaining this to Marie he said, "There have been too many changes over the sixteen-year life of the paper, one editor and owner after another. My task is to improve the paper and give it stability of management and high quality. I feel it is far better to let the paper speak for itself as it improves, rather than make promises that may not be believed."

Two weeks later the front page carried a copy of the paper's congratulatory telegram to Roald Amundsen and a long story with map to show the route the explorer had taken to make the famous Northwest Passage through the ice from the Atlantic to the Pacific. Amundsen had arrived in Egbert, Alaska with his sloop "*Gjøa.*" Amundsen's prompt and cordial reply would make another page one item the following week.

Just before Christmas the future King Haakon arrived in Kristiania and with that story there was a picture of a pretty young woman in a Hardanger-style national costume. She was the future Queen Maud, daughter of King Edward of

England, who had, before the coronation, donned the costume in Bergen and gone to a photographer to have the picture taken under the assumed name of "Miss Applegaard." Norway was ecstatic.

By the middle of January *Washington Posten* was promoting subscriptions at $1 per year, in advance, calling attention to its bringing the latest news not only from Norway and Denmark, but also from the entire civilized world. This was part of the mission Gunnar had set himself: important news about the United States and many other countries in the language most familiar to his readers. In all cases Gunnar had rewritten and translated the articles from other media.

There were far fewer Danes than Norwegians on the West Coast. In those years the written language – in Norway as well as in *Washington Posten* – was Dano-Norwegian. This would change over the next years as the spirit of nationalism in Norway moved the language away from the Danish influence and closer to what was seen as the historic Norwegian spelling and pronunciation. Under Gunnar's leadership *Washington Posten* would be one of the first Norwegian-American newspapers to keep abreast of that change. With the growing spirit of Norwegian nationalism, Gunnar decreased and eventually ended the attempt to serve the relatively few Danish-American readers.

Washington Posten may have been unique among Norwegian-American newspapers in that it commenced its publication in the same typeface used in American daily newspapers. Virtually all other Norwegian-American newspapers used the old-fashioned "German" type, heavy in curlicues and by today's standards very difficult to read. However, *WashingtonPosten's* modern appearance was not intentional.

When Frank Oleson went to Portland, Oregon in early 1889 to purchase printing equipment for the paper he planned to start on Norway's Constitution Day, the Seventeen of May, there was no "German type" in stock. He had to apologize to his readers for the "Latin" or everyday American typeface *Washington Posten* used. But what was a hardship for some readers in those early days was a blessing for the writer of this book who, just weeks before the calendar read 2000, was reading the old files of *Washington Posten* by microfiche reader. Had the paper been printed in "German" type the task would have been nearly impossible.

Gunnar's innovations came one after another in his early years. First, he was able to find over much of the Pacific Coast area regular correspondents who met weekly deadlines, sending in news items about events and people in their areas. This made it possible to attract more subscribers. Second, he greatly increased the number of exchange papers coming eventually from almost all parts of Norway and making it possible to build the weekly news coverage of Norway. It would be almost a quarter of a century before Norway would set up a press bureau serving Norwegian-American papers by wireless. Third, he built news sources in all the many Norwegian churches and organizations in the Seattle area and, to a lesser extent, in other West Coast communities. Fourth, he traveled all over the West Coast when there was an opportunity to cover worthy meetings and meet prospective subscribers. Finally, he helped convince Seattle businessmen of the growing importance of the Norwegian-American market, which resulted in substantial increases in paid advertising.

Also within the first few years, he added Severin Reinholdtsen to the business staff as a commissioned traveling subscription solicitor. Reinholdtsen systematically worked the outlying Norwegian population areas, and thereby made a living for his family and poured in a growing number of new subscribers, renewals, and what he called "payups" - payment by overdue subscribers who had failed to respond to mailed bills. In 1911 Reinholdtsen became advertising manager of the paper, a position he held for over 20 years.

With all the changes he introduced to the paper, Gunnar himself was changing. He was still working long hours, but he was getting more done. From his first days of troubled concentration on writing and filling the paper, he now found much of the work routine and fairly easy. He was no longer the "fumbler" he had considered himself at first. His expertise was growing and he now had time to think about the role of a Norwegian language newspaper and, necessarily, the role he had to play.

He realized that for many of his readers, both rural and urban, *Washington Posten* might be the only "general" newspaper they would be reading. That put the burden on his paper to give them a picture of what was happening in the world and, especially, in the United States.

He also felt he had a responsibility to help all his readers become successful in America and, even more important, to help them become good and participating citizens of the United States. To fulfill those responsibilities it was necessary to give the readers useful information on current political matters, recommendations on voting and information on becoming a citizen,

Unquestionably, readers looked to *Washington Posten* to give them news of what was going on among their countrymen not only in the Seattle area but also throughout the West Coast states, and, especially, what was happening in Norway.

Taking all of this into consideration, the early development of *Washington Posten* and of Gunnar as editor indicated that he set up a schedule of editorial priorities that determined position on page one, assuming equal importance of the individual stories. But this was no straightjacket. The subjective element might count more than standard priority weighting if a story had unusual human appeal or outstanding significance that might warrant precedence. He considered the right-hand column on page one as the top or most important position, left-hand column as second most important and, after the paper went to seven columns, fourth or center column as the third priority position.

All this told him what he had to become. As a sifter and judge of news value, he had to be making decisions constantly and quickly. This required him to hold a clear picture of his objectives. And all this standard weighting had to be balanced against what his subscribers needed and wanted and also what would help the paper appeal to a wider circle of readers.

He saw this required, and was beginning to shape, a change in him. Not too many years before he had been struggling to make a living as a newcomer immigrant. He had found a long sequence of hard labor jobs and struggled to do them well enough to be able to hold them.

Now, after his quick apprenticeship as a journalist without a mentor to coach him any longer, he was struggling again; but this time the stakes were much higher. He knew it was a matter of survival. He could not afford to fail. He read the Norwegian-American exchange papers with heightened attention, looking for ideas he could adopt. When he had put the paper to bed each Wednesday evening, it was not unusual for him to have a sleepless night, worrying about what could have been done better, what was undone, and how he could avoid the same pitfall next week.

Gradually the tension abated. Things were improving, not only in the paper itself, but also in his self-appraisal as editor. He did not question now that Frank Oleson and Marie had both been correct in insisting *Washington Posten* was the career for him. It was now his life. He felt that during the years before he had been a lost soul searching for an identity. Now, he was Gunnar Lund, publisher and editor trying with increasing success to make sure his readers and his community had reason to agree that he had earned that title.

***

In *Washington Posten* for March 2, 1906 a letter appeared from Marie V. Lund, reporting that during a fall visit to her relatives in Chicago she had attended a meeting of the (Norwegian-American) Children's Home Society and was much interested in its work. "In hope we can organize a similar society here where there are many needy children" she invited interested persons to come forward. Within a few months *Barnevenen*, The Children's Friend, was born with Marie as first president. Through her leadership it would mature into a major Norwegian-American effort in the years to come.

The death of Stavanger novelist Alexander Kielland was reported on March 9, "another one of Norway's great men." On April 20 a large picture with accompanying article about the earthquake and fire was headlined "San Francisco in Ruins." Three weeks later *Washington Posten* reported the death of Henrik Ibsen, the renowned Norwegian playwright whose fame was worldwide.

Frank Oleson, "one of our leading Norwegian attorneys," made the news again in late April when he was billed as main speaker for the Leif Erickson and Valkyrien lodges of the Sons and Daughters of Norway Seventeenth of May program in Seattle.

The 47-ton, 73-foot long sloop Gjøa with Roald Amundsen and his crew came to Seattle from Alaska on September 21 after navigating the Northwest Passage. Gunnar pulled all the stops to give a detailed description of "this inspiring visitor" and his warm reception in Seattle.

On the editorial page Gunnar launched a blistering attack on the *Seattle Times* interview with Amundsen, suggesting the *Times* did not really know the difference between Norway and Sweden and jabbed the *Times* again in mentioning "its too long history as a Seattle newspaper." In later years he could be equally upset, but he learned to repress such small expressions of his own anger.

A major story of the following year, 1907, was the presentation by the Norwegian *Storting* (parliament) of the Nobel Peace Prize to President Theodore Roosevelt.

In April Gunnar gave front-page coverage to the destruction by fire of the huge Port Blakeley mill on Puget Sound where he had worked briefly loading lumber on a schooner when he first came to Seattle in 1889.

On May Seventeenth, the birthday of *Washington Posten*, Gunnar had a playful editorial comment on changes he had made in the newspaper and set a goal for the future. He wrote that he did not expect *Washington Posten* would be the only Norwegian-Danish newspaper on the Pacific Coast, but he was determined it would be the best. Actually, he achieved both mileposts over time, for though Norwegian newspapers were started in many West Coast cities, over three dozen competitive publications in the Puget Sound area alone, *Washington Posten* was the only one that survived. He wrote that he was pleased with reader comments and delighted with the congratulations he received on the paper's eighteenth birthday, his second year as editor.

Gunnar at work in the Washington Posten's *one-room office —*
First Avenue at Cherry Street, Seattle, about 1907.

He had recently changed from a six-column page to full seven columns. Another major change was being planned. Since its inception the paper has been set by hand, with a crew of printers picking out each individual letter. The result was a print shop that represented by far the largest single cost item. Gunnar knew that the new linotype method would require only one operator with potential for greatly reducing costs. The move toward such a system was only feasible if Gunnar could find a Norwegian linotype operator. Furthermore, he wished to get the printing itself entirely out of his business so he could concentrate his time on newsgathering, editing, subscriptions and advertising. Within some months he found the perfect custom printing company and a trained Norwegian linotype operator. The result was significantly reduced cost, as well as a sizable reduction in time spent on activities he did not consider "my real business, which is editing a better newspaper."

No longer needing a print shop of his own, Gunnar moved his office to smaller quarters in the Washington Building at First Avenue and Cherry Street. This gave another reduction in operating costs and helped make the paper more profitable so he could add an assistant editor in the future.

That year's big Seattle Seventeenth of May celebration was held at Broadway Hall with Consul Thomas Kolderup giving the welcoming address and Pastor C. August Peterson giving the main address. Rev. Peterson's speech, in full, was reported in the next week's paper together with his picture.

Gunnar had the ability and courage to be critical when the occasion called for it. He attended the unveiling of the Wergeland Statue at Fargo, North Dakota and his story on the event was an example of how sharp his pencil could be. Between four and five thousand persons were present to honor the man who more than any other kindled the nationalist movement that culminated in the writing of the Norwegian constitution in 1814. One of the great Norwegian-American writers Waldemar Ager was the speaker and he was honored by rapt attention. But of six speakers, he was the only one who spoke in Norwegian. The whole affair was too much dominated "by the chamber of commerce crowd" according to Gunnar, who wrote the celebration was "not Norwegian enough." There were no Norwegian flags in evidence; the band played no Norwegian music. The Sons of Norway lodge that sponsored the affair "forgot its duty."

On September 27 the paper carried a major page one picture and story regarding the death of Edvard Grieg with considerable treatment on his international reputation and the "Norwegianism" of his great music.

In May 1909 the paper printed a letter from the Parkland

Children's Home, thanking *Barnevenen* (The Children's Friend) for a $125 new stove and other goods which came at the absolute moment of greatest need – the bottom had fallen out of the old stove the day before the new stove was delivered.

The year of 1909 was devoted to preparation for the Alaska Yukon Pacific World Fair in Seattle. Work was progressing on a Viking ship being built in Bothell, near Seattle, and the large Norwegian committee chaired by H. P. Rude was working feverishly to make Norway Day the outstanding event of the fair. The committee, Gunnar reported, was "dreaming great dreams."

The "great dreams" were fulfilled, as the paper proudly stated in a later issue, pointing to Norway Day's scoring the fair's largest attendance. Thousands watched the arrival of the Viking ship with its appropriately garbed and armed crew and a Viking queen, the six golden haired Valkyrie on three white and three black horses, a bridal procession with two bridal couples and a fiddler all in national costume. Another popular feature was "the Eidsvold men" representing the signing of the constitution in 1814. The band from St. Olaf College in Northfield, Minnesota played. Norwegian Consul Kolderup was the speaker and there was a message from King Haakon VII that was read to the assemblage with great applause.

As Gunnar remarked editorially in his September 3 edition, "At Norway Day the Norwegian banner was borne higher than it has ever been borne in America. The American press has given us similar praise." The final attendance figures compared to that of the next two highest contenders: German Day 38,642, Swedish Day 40,352, and Norway Day 42,026.

In October President Taft visited Seattle and *Washington Posten*, true to its Republican stance, gave him a hearty welcome to the city and state.

On May 6, 1910 the paper reported that "All of Norway is a folk in sorrow. Over all the country flags are at half-mast observing the death of Bjørnstjerne Bjørnson in Paris. A Norwegian naval ship will bring the body home to burial."

Bjørnson, of all Norway's many great authors, was the one most beloved by the people. He had justly been called a genius and the "uncrowned king of Norway." He had dominated Norwegian culture and politics until his death. He had applied his restless energy and had become a poet, a theatre director, a playwright, a truly beloved author, and the writer of the poem that became the national anthem. He was also a gadfly and demonstrated this on his tour of the United States in 1880-1881 by attacking the role of the Norwegian Lutheran Church and the "somnolence" of Norwegian-Americans.

Gunnar was gratified to see a cause he had championed personally finally winning approval in the independent Sons of Norway of the West Coast. It joined the older and much larger Midwest organization headquartered in Minneapolis to become District 2, Sons of Norway International. In 1910 District 2 included British Columbia, all the Pacific Norwest states and the states of the Southwest, including California.

News from the Ballard area was carried in columns devoted to "Coast News." Ballard did not become part of Seattle until its annexation in 1907, but it was already a center for Norwegian fishermen and had its own separate Seventeenth of May celebration and its own Normanna Male Chorus. Many years later it became the acknowledged "capital" for Norwegian-Americans in the Seattle area. Ballard also became the home of *Western Viking* (the successor to *Washington Posten*), the site of Bergen Square, the Leif Erickson monument, and the location of the largest Seventeenth of May celebrations in the West.

In March 1911 the paper reported that Scott and Amundsen had both landed in the Antarctic and there was an obvious race to reach the South Pole. The biggest news of 1912 for *Washington Posten* was that Roald Amundsen had won the race to the pole and was the official discoverer. This news commanded front space with a large picture of Amundsen.

Editorially Gunnar declared, "With this new victory Amundsen has become our time's most famous explorer. Luck? No! Practical good sense and unyielding will!"

New data from the 1910 census, published in 1912, revealed that there were 23,363 persons living in Washington State who were born in Norway.

The masthead in December carried the name K. A. Kleppe as the editorial secretary (or assistant editor). Gunnar put extra effort in training the new man so that he could be trusted to run the paper for an extended time in 1914. Gunnar was planning to be in Norway that year for the centennial of the signing of the Norwegian constitution. He had less than two years to bring Kleppe up to a point where he could be trusted to edit and manage the paper for over five months while Gunnar was away.

In connection with the coming Constitution Day Centennial in Norway, there was a great effort among Norwegian-Americans all over the United States to collect money for a "remembrance gift" to Norway. *Washington Posten* carried a weekly reminder of the proposed gift and asked its readers to contribute, noting that the paper was accredited to receive and receipt for such gifts.

The June 6 issue was fairly typical. The first page carried the weekly Norway letter that was continued on the editorial page, page four. There was a three-column front page story with pictures of delegates to the annual meeting of the

Norwegian Lutheran Free Church, a one-column story on Germany and its brittle relations with other European countries, a one-column speculation on whom President Wilson would appoint as minister to Norway, and a one-column story on the "invisible lobby" in Washington D.C. To make sure no favoritism was being shown, a following issue would carry a major story on the annual meeting of the Norwegian Lutheran Synod.

Chapter 6

WAR YEARS

Washington Posten always carried full news coverage on District Grand Lodge annual meetings of the Sons and Daughters of Norway and equally strong coverage on annual *Sangerfests* of the Norwegian Male Chorus. Gunnar attended these events whenever possible, not only to write the necessary news stories but also, as he said to Marie, to "show the flag" for *WashingtonPosten*. He rarely returned to his Seattle office without having signed up new subscribers and having received renewal payments from current subscribers.

In Norway there was an ongoing debate as to whether *Riksmål* (national language) or *Landsmål* (country language) deserved to get the upper hand in the ongoing move from Dano-Norwegian to a "pure" Norwegian language. *Landsmål* was a combination of regional dialects into a merged form.

Washington Posten voted strongly for *Riksmål*, while happily printing in pure country language the full Seattle speech by Pastor Anders Hovden at the affair commemorating the 100th anniversary of the birth of Iver Åsen, the father of *Landsmål*. Later, *Landsmål* would develop into its successor *Nynorsk* or New Norwegian.

On Lincoln's birthday in 1914 Gunnar's editorial declared "we recognize he is the greatest of all the sons of the United States with pride for his contribution to mankind's

Marie and Gunnar — Seattle 1914.

pilgrimage on this earth." A few weeks later under the heading "Danger for Civilization" there was a full column on the ominous situation between Germany and Great Britain. But in Berlin, Nina Grieg, widow of the Norwegian composer, attended the opening night of Ibsen's *Peer Gynt* at the Royal Theatre. The orchestra played Grieg's *Peer Gynt Suite*. Nina was invited to have breakfast with the Kaiser who presented her with a huge bouquet of roses.

A red-letter day for the Lund family was April 17, 1914. Gunnar, Marie and the three children left for Norway on a trip that would take in all the massive festivities of the centennial of the signing of the Norwegian Constitution and include many side trips to visit relatives. Friends saw them off at the train station, and a delegation from Valkyrien Lodge, Daughters of Norway, presented a bouquet of roses to Marie, a charter member and past president of the lodge.

Gunnar wrote a front-page story, usually several columns long, for almost all issues of the paper from the day of his

Enroute to Norway: Gunnar with Roald, Marie Lund, Mabel, Amalie and Haakon Vognild, John and Helga Lund — Chicago 1914.

departure until the family returned from Norway in early September. His weekly stories were headlined "Norway in Holiday and Workday." They carried the byline "By Gunnar Lund, Editor." This was the first time he used that title since he had taken over the paper nine years earlier. In the first of these stories mailed from Chicago, he told of his having been in the United States for 22 years, wanting to see Norway again, and how wonderful it was to be going home with Marie and the three children. He added that the children had behaved amazingly well during the three days and nights of the long train trip, even including the youngest, two-year old Roald.

They stopped in Chicago to visit the Vognild family. Marie's Uncle Erik had passed away but her Aunt Amalie was in good health and she with the Lunds attended the wedding of her daughter Selma to Harry Forbes. Amelie Vognild, her son Haakon and daughter Mabel accompanied the Lunds to Norway.

The same issue of the paper ran a story on the collection of funds for a centennial remembrance gift to Norway. The total to date was $41,173.65, made up of gifts as small as fifty cents or a dollar from thousands of Norwegian-Americans. It had been decided that the gift would be "lost" if presented during the busy centennial celebration on the Seventeenth of May and therefore to present it on the American Independence Day, July 4. The final total was close to 250,000 kroner.

From New York Gunnar wrote of Sons of Norway District 3 festivities for voyagers to the centennial in Norway. Gunnar represented and brought greetings from West Coast District 2.

Back home, Kleppe, the assistant editor of *Washington Posten*, did an enthusiastic job of reporting the Seventeenth of May in Seattle. He stated that the celebration was an outstanding, magnificent proof that when Norwegian-American organizations worked together they could produce the most beautiful, most moving Constitution Day festivals that have ever been held in the city. He supported the story with pictures of the large parade in Volunteer Park.

Aboard the *Bergensfjord* of the Norwegian America Line, Gunnar participated with the welcoming speech in a program conducted in all three sections of the ship on April 21 and 22. Marie Lund recited Bjørnstjerne Bjørnson's *"Bergljot."* For Gunnar boarding the ship was one of his proudest moments. He was sailing to Norway in Norway's own ship! He had been a staunch and active supporter of organizing the Norwegian America Line from the first moment.

Arriving in Norway, Gunnar sent home a six-column story about the Seventeenth of May in Kristiania and a whirlwind of festivities. This was followed by a report on the festivities in Eidsvoll where the constitution was written in 1814, and then the festivities at the great Nidaros Cathedral

Anna Wiggen (Marie's sister) and her two daughters Maisa and Aslaug — Brekstad, Ørlandet, Norway 1914.

in Trondheim that dates from the early Middle Ages. At that time it was undergoing a lengthy process of reconstruction.

From Trondheim the Lunds traveled to Brekstad at Ørlandet to visit with Marie's sister Anna Wiggen and her husband Simon. While there Helga was taken by her two cousins Aslaug and Maisa to the village store. On the way home they met a group of gypsies who wanted to touch Helga's golden blond hair. The girls ran home in fright.

The family next journeyed into the mountains to Oppdal for a reunion with the Dørum, Viken and Vognild families, then to Stavanger on the southwest seacoast, where Gunnar had a reunion with his brother Gustav Abrahamsen. It will be remembered that Abrahamsen was the family name Gunnar jettisoned when he came to America. Gustav had come from Sweden where he was head of a curtain manufacturing plant.

The last days of visiting in Norway were dampened by serious concern. World War I had broken out. When the family sailed August 20 from Kristiania on the *Stavangerfjord* she was carrying over a thousand Norwegian-Americans who were trying to get home. The Lunds returned to Seattle on September 2, 1914.

Gunnar's articles from Norway mirrored the depth of his feeling and the joy of seeing the old country once again. He wrote from the heart and yet with the critical eye of a journalist. What he saw, he liked. He knew why he and so many hundreds of thousands of other emigrants had left home. They went primarily for opportunity that was denied them in Norway, and most of them found it in the United States and Canada, but they never forgot the beauty of Norway, its fjords, its mountains, and their own people. To read his weekly articles was to experience with him a sense of homecoming, the fulfillment of years of waiting and longing.

Now that he was home in Seattle again, he reviewed the issues of his paper from the week he left to the week he returned. He thanked young Kleppe, "You have done very well! I hope we have many years of working together." That hope, however, was not to be realized. Within a few months Kleppe returned to Norway. His replacement was a name that would become as closely tied to *Washington Posten* as that of Gunnar Lund. He was O. L. Ejde. He had taken a break for several years while he experienced the great adventure of being a crewmember on Capt. Hvatum's halibut schooner, *Scandia* and for a short time he worked as a logger. Ejde (pronounced A-dah, with a long A) never used his first name, Ole. He was a hard- working, immensely competent assistant editor. His name and contribution will come up later when our chronicle reaches the 40's and he becomes editor and, for some years, publisher.

What became known by many as "Seattle's Norwegian colony" went into an orbit of celebration on the Seventeenth of May in 1915. The May 21 issue of *Washington Posten* had a three column picture of the beautiful reason: the new Norway Hall built by the Sons & Daughters of Norway lodges at the corner of Boren Avenue and Virginia Street.

Traditional Norwegian dragons looked down from the four peaks of the roof. The building was entirely of wood and there was no question as to where its inspiration lay: *Det var ekte norsk!* (It was authentic Norwegian). No one could mistake the origin of its architecture. While the outside commanded attention, the inside was equally appealing. The local Norwegian artist Yngvar Sonnichsen had painted huge traditional Norwegian murals in rich, muted tones. One excited observer said, "This is Norway with a true 1800s flavor. It's magnificent!"

The pleased Norwegian-American colony felt the same. It was more than a place for the Sons and Daughters to hold their monthly meetings. It became the home of their big fall bazaars, the preferred meeting place for all types of Norwegian organizations and weekly dances. It was the attractive visual symbol of all things Norwegian in Seattle, Years later, with the heavy geographical shift of Seattle-area Norwegians, it became (minus many of the typical Norwegian touches) the home of the Painter's Union. A new "Norway Center" was then established in what was to become the Seattle Center area. Much later a new Leif Erikson hall was built in Ballard.

One weekly feature in the news indicated *Washington Posten* was beginning to reach beyond the Rocky Mountains. Titled *Vesterheimen*, (The Western Home), the traditional name used by the early Norwegian settlers in the prairie states, the paper included news from Iowa, the Dakotas, Minnesota,

Illinois, Wisconsin and other major Midwest settlements.

During August 1915 the paper carried heavy news coverage of the war, commenting there had been one year of war and no peace was in sight.

The Children's Friend took on a larger mission and a new name: The Norwegian Hospital Association. Its long-term goal was to establish a new hospital in Seattle. As a fund raiser, it scheduled a "Tour Norway By Auto" program, with cars leaving Norway Hall from 2 to 5 on August 13 to a series of Norwegian homes, then returning for supper at the Hall for only 25 cents.

Norway Hall became the site of the Sons and Daughters of Norway lutefisk, lefse and rommegrøt dinner October 8 and bazaar for five days in November.

The major news story on January 21, 1916 told of the city of Bergen being devastated by a fire that left 20,000 homeless. Many buildings destroyed. When the north Pacific halibut fleet went on strike in March there was a seven column headline plus picture, an indication of the interest the Norwegian colony felt for this almost totally Norwegian-manned halibut fishing fleet.

Editorially the paper commented on the very special conditions under which the Seventeenth of May was celebrated in a Norway that was struggling to defend its neutrality. The outlook was grim with German subs prowling off shore and attacking Norwegian shipping,

On April 1, 1917, *Washington Posten* moved its offices to rooms 923-924 in the new Seaboard Building at the corner of Fourth Avenue and Pike Street. This was to be the address of the paper for many years and it shortened the distance from the office to the Lund home at 1021 Summit Avenue North to almost exactly two miles. Gunnar walked the distance morning and night except in stubborn downpours or a heavy snow. It was his daily "constitutional" that did so much to keep him in trim condition despite his sedentary desk job.

In our nation's capitol the draft was passed and signed by President Wilson on April 6, 1917. June 5 was set as registration day.

On May 25 Gunnar's editorial was headed "The Shame of It" in which he described an editorial run by the *Seattle Star* headed "The Nerve of It" It dealt with a Norwegian-Swedish joint mission to Washington D.C. to protest the existing U.S. embargo on foodstuffs. "They (Norway and Sweden) continue to sell Germany nickel and other metals which the Germans will use to kill us Americans, while the Swedes and Norwegians expect us to keep their tables loaded with food."

The *Washington Posten* editorial called this an unfounded rumor and accused *The Star* of blithely ignoring the mounting Norwegian merchant marine losses caused by German subs. "It doesn't surprise us. *The Star's* powers of discrimination are just as limited as its respect for fair play is small."

Though the United States was at war, the West Coast *Sangerfest* in Seattle scheduled to start August 31 and run through September 3, was held at the Masonic Temple and was publicized by an advertisement that covered the top twelve inches of the main Seattle news page. The following week the five-column headline, story and picture on page one reported on the event.

It was in October 1917 that all foreign-language newspapers in the United States were required to use English exclusively for any reports or editorials regarding the conduct of the war. *Washington Posten* of course complied. The paper was requesting a permit to use Norwegian for war items and, as difficult as English might be for some of

*Marie Lund in her Liberty Loan
speaker's outfit — Seattle 1918.*

its readers, asked them to be patient until permission was granted. Reader complaints were few. By December 28 the paper began carrying a top of page one banner which read:

"Published and distributed under Permit No. 310, authorized by act October 6 on file at the Post Office Seattle, Wash. By order of the President, A.S. Burleson, Postmaster General."

Gunnar ran that banner for months after the paper was authorized to resume publishing war news in Norwegian. He obviously felt the statement had some value in defusing the anti-foreign-language press sentiment.

English language war reports and editorials indicated how successful Gunnar's "homework" had been in perfecting his English from the days when he was a raw immigrant and through the intervening years. He used his new skills with confidence and competence.

The columns of *Washington Posten* during the late spring and summer continuing into the fall of 1918, were full of news about Norwegian-American support for the American war effort. All the Norwegian churches had Red Cross Auxiliaries producing garments and bandages. *Washington Posten* devoted editorial and advertising space in a consistent, vigorous campaign for the Liberty Loans.

Marie Lund participated in the war support effort of her church, Immanuel Lutheran, and also was a volunteer speaker for the Liberty Loans, traveling constantly by streetcar, jitney (unofficial taxis), train and bus in her Red Cross costume all over the King County area. She was to receive a citation for her work after the end of the war.

In December Gunnar commented on an editorial that had appeared in the *Seattle Post-Intelligencer*. The *P-I* had stated, "There is no pressing need to organize associations to keep alive fatherland languages and customs. Most of our immigrants came to this country to get away from all that. The more rapidly the European immigrant becomes American in language, sentiment and devotion, that much better off we all are."

To this, *Washington Posten* responded in English, "The *P-I* is wrong both as to the cause of the European immigration and as to the benefits that would accrue to America in case the immigrant followed its advice. American sentiment supporting the high ideals America stands for is not dependent on birthplace. Many immigrants came to these shores better Americans in every respect than those born here of Mayflower extraction. And we must wish them to retain their interest in the land of their birth. It would indeed be a poor acquisition to our citizenship if our newcomers were mere numbers to be added to our population. And we believe that a man knowing and cultivating two or more languages in most cases will be more desirable and valuable to his new fatherland than one who knows only one."

The attack on things "foreign" in the United States mounted in a wartime wave of hysteria. Perhaps this helps explain a decision made by the Norwegian Lutheran Church. *Washington Posten's* June 21 editorial lamented the happening. The item is translated from the original Norwegian, as are all *Washington Posten* items unless otherwise indicated:

"Many will read with sorrow the resolution from the meeting in Fargo, North Dakota regarding changing the name of the Norwegian Lutheran Church. It must be approved by two-thirds majority in a meeting two years from now. The Fargo vote of 533 to 61 makes it obvious how that vote will go.

"We must openly state that we cannot admit as valid the thinking that the Norwegian Lutheran Church should strip itself of every trace of its origin.

"To us it looks like the resolution is a disclosure that under the prevailing hysteria (the Church) people have taken flight. In this connection, Governor Harding of Iowa is reported as saying, "I am telling those who support foreign languages that the Good Lord above is (only) listening to voices in English."

Washington Posten on January 18, 1918 carried news of the House passing a bill to grant voting rights for women. In the same issue it reported Red Cross needs and estimated that 10,000 women were involved in volunteer work for the Red Cross in King and Kitsap counties alone with 300 auxiliaries active.

On February 15 the paper reported that food rationing

was expected to begin in Norway where prices were soaring because of the German blockade on shipping. In July it reported that a German submarine had sunk the Norwegian ship *Kong Raud* off the northern coast of Norway. By September 6, 1918 the tide seemed to be running against the Germans and it was reported they were taking heavy losses. Russia's withdrawal from the war had freed the German forces on the eastern front to join the western front but their addition was more than compensated for by the increasing number of American soldiers fighting there. Editorially, *Washington Posten* said *La oss slå til!* "Let's hit 'em!"

In Iowa Americans of Norwegian origin were amazed and disappointed over the intolerance of their Governor W.L. Harding who proclaimed a ban on all spoken use of foreign languages in schools, churches, public places and in all public address. "Let those who cannot speak or understand the English language conduct their religious worship in their homes," he was quoted as saying. *Washington Posten* declared the governor's proclamation unconstitutional and a departure from the American tradition of protecting minorities against attack by the majority.

Wartime did not completely stifle entertainment in Seattle. The paper reported that Rolf and Dagny Hammer of New York were appearing in Ibsen's "A Doll's House" at Norway Hall on September 14 and November 30. Marie Lund was playing a part. Tickets ranged from 75 cents to $1. The Hammers came back to Seattle in May of the following year to present Ibsen's "Master Builder."

On November 11, 1918, after four and a half years, the war came to an end. A few weeks later *Washington Posten* reminded that the fifth Liberty Loan was in full swing, and recommended all readers support it.

Norwegian-Americans hailed the death of the Minnesota

Warner bill that would have required all foreign-language newspapers to provide full English translations of every issue. The argument that killed the bill in committee was that enactment would destroy the foreign-language press, the most effective means of communicating Americanism to many of the foreign born. Gunnar breathed a sigh of relief, but wondered where the anti-foreign born menace would strike next.

In May 1919, just after the muted Seventeenth of May celebrations in Seattle, Gunnar commented editorially on the sharp difference from previous years. Goals were lower, attendance was down. He saw this as a result of the hysteria that had plagued the war years. He became aware through exchange papers that Norwegian-American festivities in the mid-west had been sharply scaled back under pressures of what was called in the Norwegian-American press the "anti-foreigner hysteria."

He welcomed to page one the message from George Creel, wartime commissioner on public information. The brief item gave thanks and sincere appreciation to the foreign-language press for its loyal, sympathetic and effective support of the war effort of the United States. Reviewing the wartime copies of *Washington Posten* would convince anyone that Gunnar had indeed done his utmost, and done it well.

But the anti-foreign-language hysteria was hardly over. The "one language" issue was alive and well. In Washington D.C. Wesley L Jones in a speech to the American Women's Suffrage Association declared it was time to insist on one language only in schools and press. A month later a bill was introduced in the U.S. Senate to forbid use of U.S. mails to any newspaper or other publication not printed in the English language. Gunnar labelled this a foolish attempt to build a

"Chinese great wall" around the U.S. He saw the hysteria as an indication of "siege or conspiracy mentality," an illusion that foreign languages and the foreign-born were attacking America. The bill was referred to committee where it died.

One of Ole Ejde's important contributions to the paper was his introduction of adequate coverage of sports news from Norway and also of Norwegian-Americans. His first major breakthrough was a three-column page one story, complete with pictures, of a ski jumping meet on Mount Rainier.

Gunnar's mid-June editorial was a defense of foreign languages and the institutions of the foreign-born; the editorial was translated into English and read in its entirety at a Carnegie Institute meeting by H. Sundby-Hansen. The meeting was called by the Institute to further research in Americanization. Many of the invited participants were editors from various foreign countries.

The *Washington Posten* editorial was entitled "Americanization" and it was a sharp criticism of the American-born population as lacking knowledge of anything outside the U.S. It was also suggested that many American-born citizens need information on the Americanization process as much as the immigrants themselves do. The American-born must learn and understand the economic and cultural values the immigrants brought to America. Americans must understand that a person cannot change his nationality as easily as he changes his shirt. The Americanization process can only be carried out with the help of institutions of the foreign born: churches, schools, and not least, by the newspapers in the immigrants' own language.

According to an article in *Stavanger Aftenblad*, Gunnar's editorial was greeted by "tumultuous applause." It also said that many of those present considered it had a deeper impact than any other contribution to the meeting.

A major finding of the conference, *Stavanger Aftenblad* declared, was the realization that one can't apply the same yardstick to every nationality involved in Americanization, and the best possible result for Americanization can only be achieved through complete cooperation with the institutions of the foreign born.

Arne Kildal, the head of the Norsemen's League (*Nordmanns Forbundet*) in Norway, referring to the editorial, predicted that the Norwegian language would be literally forgotten in the United States and Canada within a generation because Norwegian-Americans were not teaching the language to their children. In an editorial Gunnar reminded his readers that a person with two languages was better off than a person with but one language and advised his readers to teach their children Norwegian.

This was hardly in keeping with Gunnar's own practices. He and Marie rarely spoke Norwegian at home. He made it plain to his children that he wanted them to feel at home in America as Americans. Certainly he never made any effort to teach his children Norwegian. Whatever command of the language they acquired was learned in Norway during their visits there. On the other hand, there was no question but that Gunnar did show his great love and respect for Norway and that he did his best to instill the same regard for the country in his children.

The end of attacks on foreign-language newspapers was not over. At the end of January in 1920 *Washington Posten* reported that in the last minutes of the Oregon Legislature's special session a bill was introduced which would effectively make it illegal to publish, sell or distribute a newspaper or other publication printed only in a foreign language. The bill was passed and signed by the governor. The bill was introduced by Swedish-born Senator A.W. Nordblad of Astoria and two representatives of Swedish descent, Lofgren and Westerland.

Gunnar's editorial comment: "We have long known that we live in an hysteric and reactionary time. It is ironic that our sons went to Europe to fight for freedom. But at home, again, we have this mad Chinese great wall. The Oregon law allows a foreign-language newspaper to be published and distributed providing that it also prints a complete and accurate translation into English. Since this would be impossibly expensive, the law effectively prohibits distribution of a foreign-language publication in Oregon."

The Seattle American Legion Post, claiming that Americanization of immigrants was seriously delayed by foreign-language publications later sent a similar resolution to the Washington State legislators. Gunnar pointed out editorially that the Oregon law was dead, and that a similar fate could be expected in Washington. He was right.

In February of 1920 the wartime hysteria was still at work. The Norwegian Male Chorus of Portland, Oregon, voted to change its name to the Multnomah Male Chorus. Gunnar's editorial comment: Oregon seems a state where wolves and others would rather appear in lamb's clothing.

A Swiss organization in Oregon called a meeting to protest the proposed muzzling of the foreign-language press. Among the speakers was Haakon J. Langloe, publisher of *Pacific Skandinaven*, Portland's short-lived Norwegian language newspaper. He surprised the audience by attacking the Swiss protest and the foreign born in general. The speaker was reported by the Portland *Oregonian* as having characterized the foreign born as "These people who came from the old country and have continued to use its language and follow its traditions. They have created a nation within a nation and have neglected their duties to their new country."

Gunnar's editorial comment was one of amazement and disapproval. He stated the mission of every foreign-language newspaper editor was to use its native language to explain America's ideals to those who did not yet fully understand English. "It is without question our work to help the immigrant become a mature American citizen. His (Langloe's) accusations are unconscionable."

Four months later Gunnar reported that Langloe, now editor of an English-language paper, was advocating a law that would make it unlawful to publish a foreign-language newspaper anywhere in the United States.

Chapter 7

ERLAND POINT

Scratch a Norwegian city dweller and you are bound to find a longing for a cabin in the country. If you take *Hurtigruten,* the famous Norwegian Coastal Express, in the first days along the passage from Bergen to the Arctic Circle city of Tromsø your ship will pass dozens and hundreds of tiny shoreside cabins, most of them dark Norwegian red. Or go to any inland valley reasonably close to a inland city and you will find tidy cabins up in the hills.

Consider for example two retired engineers who originally came from Oppdal. They were born on *Gulsenget* (Golden Field Farm). One brother who lives in Trondheim has his cabin up on the ancestral *seter,* the mountain summer farm of the family, which is a *seter* so old and so clearly identified as historic that it is shown on the more detailed maps of the country as *Dørumsetra.*

The other brother spent his adult years in South Korea as the leader of a large engineering firm but still maintained a home in Oslo for his family, plus, quite naturally, a cabin out on Oslofjord.

These and so many other Norwegian city-dwellers have struck their blows for a limited freedom from streets and autos and workaday jobs. They have reached out to put themselves and their families into Norway's great passion:

nature. Out in the countryside they admire the views, go for hikes or ski trips, fish, swim, pick wild berries, eat country fare, and probably also get in a lick of good, sweaty work like sawing firewood or digging in a garden and touching non-city Norway – the real or *ekte Norge*. So it was with Gunnar, a city boy from Stavanger who spent so many of his days in a Seattle office.

When springtime came the year after World War I ended, Gunnar's ancestral yearning began to build up to intolerable levels. "Marie," he said, "have you ever thought it might be nice to have a cabin out on Puget Sound someplace, just a simple cabin (*ei hyte*) so you and the children could enjoy it all summer long and I could come out on weekends? Have you ever longed for something like that?"

Yes, of course she had. She was delighted with Gunnar's interest. So began the search which lasted two months. Every Sunday Gunnar and the children boarded one of the Puget Sound "boats," as the passenger and freight craft were called locally. Gunnar scouted Bainbridge Island, but found that waterfront property so close to Seattle was prohibitively high in price and far too citified. Since Gunner never owned a car, it was imperative that the cabin be within walking distance of the dock. The boat to the Poulsbo area seemed a winner, Poulsbo was already known as "Little Norway" because most of the settlers, farmers and fishermen, spoke fluent Norwegian and it was where old friends, the Nevills and the Rylands lived. But there was no suitable waterfront property on that route either.

Then a light dawned for Marie. "Gunnar!" she reminded him, "Knut and Mary Erland have a farm on the sound, somewhere near Bremerton. Isn't that what Knut told us a few years ago?"

"Of course," Gunnar beamed, "Why didn't I think of that.

I'll call him now."

He knew Knut well, for Knut too was from Stavanger.

On a Sunday morning later that month Gunnar, Marie and the three children took the Summit streetcar downtown, transferred to the Madison Street cable car and walked the final two blocks to Colman dock. The children, going ahead, stopped expectantly at the door to the dock store. Gunnar nodded and went in to buy the customary big bag of peanuts in the shell. That had become an established habit for any trip on a Puget Sound steamer. They were on their way to Sunday dinner with the Erlands and, what was of the highest importance, to see some land on which they might build their cabin.

Boarding the *F. G. Reeve*, they started the two-hour trip with numerous stops at docks on the south end of Bainbridge Island and the winding passage in to Bremerton before turning northwest through the long Port Washington Narrows where the boat finally entered Dyes Inlet. The irregular bay was about six miles long and over a mile wide, tapering down sharply at both the north and south ends. The boat stopped at Tracyton then crossed the bay westward toward the Erland Point dock.

They saw the dock jutting out from the north side of a wide graveled point. At the base of the point a large American flag flew from a tall white flagpole. Beyond the point and up a slight rise was a white bungalow with a covered porch that spanned the width of the house. The shore to the north and south of the single visible house was wooded right down to the beach.

Knut Erland and his grandchildren, Tom and Jane, were on the dock to meet the Lund family as they disembarked. The *Reeve* tooted its whistle; the captain rang the engine room signal for slow ahead, and the boat pulled away from the dock as it headed diagonally across the bay toward Fairview and Silverdale and finally to its home port Chico.

Knut, his handsome white beard rippling in the breeze, pointed to a spot a few hundred feet south of the dock. "You see those two big old fir trees? That's the best lot we have, a hundred feet of waterfront, a full acre and a half. We'll walk down there later, but let's go up to the house to see Mary first."

Mary was out on the front porch to meet them, and she and Marie embraced. She then turned to Gunnar and shook hands, welcoming them all to Erland Point. Tom and Jane took John, Helga and Roald to see the barn, the hayfield, the chicken coop, the pump house, the orchard and other elements of the farm. Mary and Marie went into the kitchen to bring out the coffee. Knut and Gunnar sat on the front porch and talked of Stavanger, of Knut's enjoyment of retirement and the farm and eventually of the lot and the price: eight hundred dollars.

In Gunnar's way of thinking this was a reasonable figure, and he saw no reason to attempt to bargain with his old friend. He started to write a check, but Knut cautioned him, "You never close a business deal without examining the merchandise. Wait until you see whether it's worth the price."

"Knut," Gunnar asked, "How much do you pay for your subscription to *Washington Posten*?"

"Why, it must be a dollar a year, isn't it?" Knut answered.

"Exactly," said Gunnar, "You pay the asked price, I expect to do the same."

They both laughed. Knut drew a Chesterfield cigarette from the round tin can and Gunnar struck a match, lit Knut's cigarette then lit his own pipe. They sat back talking about their early days in Stavanger and about business in Seattle where Knut had been a partner in the city's largest ship chandler firm.

Mary's dinner was fricasseed chicken and small Norwegian-style dumplings with a berry pie made from the farm's own crop. This was the kind of gathering Marie would describe with the word *koselig* which the Norwegian-English dictionary defines as "cozy." But that is a literal and inadequate translation for Marie's meaning which was much broader and included the warm hospitality, the camaraderie of old friends, the babble of children's happy voices, and the aroma and flavor of home-cooked fare.

Later they walked down the beach to the property Knut had pointed out from the dock. Marie immediately noted the many wild huckleberry bushes, the tall firs, and some trees she had never seen before. They had reddish bark and green leaves. She asked Mary what they were. "That is Madrona," Mary advised. "It is an evergreen tree that I think grows only here on the north Pacific Coast. The red bark peels off in the late summer to show a green bark below. It is a very hard wood, hard to saw or split when it is dry but easy when it is fresh cut. It is very beautiful, don't you think?" Marie nodded enthusiastically, and then pointed to a spot just behind the last Madrona. "Gunnar, there is where the cabin should be, right there. From the porch we will have a fine view of the water. Is that the right place?"

Gunnar agreed and then frowned, "But Marie, even if we start building today, we probably can't move in before summer is almost over."

Knut listened, then asked, "Do you want to get out here as soon as possible?"

Marie and Gunnar both nodded.

"Well then," Knut continued, "Wait until next spring to build here and you can enjoy all next summer in your new cabin. But you can still be at Erland to enjoy most of what's left of this summer." He turned to Gunnar's oldest son,

"John, how old are you now?"

"I'll be 17 next December, Mr. Erland," John replied. Too formal? Not a bit, it was how Gunnar and Marie had trained all three of their children.

"Have you taken manual training in school?"

"Yes sir," John answered.

"Fine," Knut turned to Gunnar. "I have a man who tends the farm while we are in Seattle. He can knock together a summer camp down by the flagpole. Within two weeks you can be camping there. In the meantime, John can live with us and help put the camp together. How does that sound."

Gunnar smiled broadly and turned to Marie, "Does that have your blessing?" Marie was enthusiastic. Back at the farmhouse, she sat down with Knut to draw up plans for the first temporary camp that would give them two full months at Erland before school started the day after Labor Day.

When the family returned two weeks later, they moved into the camp. It was certainly not the same as having their own cabin on their own land. They had to use the Erland's outdoor privy and carry water from the Erland's pump house. But these little inconveniences did not bother them. They had a wonderful summer.

On the next Christmas Day the Lund family was invited to the Erland's big house on Queen Anne Hill in Seattle for dinner. Marie brought along the rough plan for the cabin to be built on their Erland property. Knut and Mary examined the plan and pronounced it excellent. It was to be ready for occupancy by the time school was out in the middle of June.

During the next spring vacation period Earl Lawson, another Erland grandson of John's age, came from Idaho for the week. He and John disassembled the camp and with major help from Knut's handyman, freighted the lumber by rowboat over to the Lund property, cleared away a few trees and some underbrush, and started construction.

The cabin was "early primitive." It was 16 by 30 feet with a front porch of the same size. It was built of lapped shiplap with a simple floor of the same material and a shingled roof over the house portion. A canvas fly covered the porch and there was a tent on the south end of the porch. The building was never painted inside or out; the interior was never paneled. Built only for summer use, it was not insulated, though that did not stop Gunnar from coming out to the cabin even during fall and winter weekends. There was a kitchen and three bedrooms for the parents, Helga, and Roald, plus the tent for John. The huge front porch under the canvas fly was the living room.

The family discovered some unanticipated benefits. At low tide, the exposed sandy beach was a harvest area for abundant small, tender white butter clams. Clam nectar and clam chowder and steamed clams were enjoyed frequently. Often on a Sunday morning Marie would remind the boys she was expecting company from Seattle for dinner. They would ask her how many were coming and then take shovels, an appropriate container, and go clamming. If a big group was expected they used a wash tub, for any smaller group just a bucket or two. The clams were so plentiful they found it easy to fill a 12-quart bucket in ten to fifteen minutes.

This wondrous bounty did not diminish even when there were more and more families at Erland Point, but in the early thirties commercial clam diggers came during the winter and totally stripped the beaches despite vigorous objection from Knut Erland. They left no clams to re-seed the beaches. Much the same happened to the trout which lurked in a "pool" a quarter-mile north of the dock. The boys would go trolling, boating a one-helping trout with each pass over the pool area. This too was to end when the purse seiners came and netted hundreds of trout in one casting of their net. That brought an end to rowboat trolling.

There were several major events the family frequently discussed in "remember when" sessions. One was the building of the privy among the trees farther up the gentle rise from the cabin. They named it for one of Seattle's popular restaurants of the day: the privy became "The Boulevard Inn." Another was finding an official- appearing sign the younger son found during beachcombing. It had apparently floated in from the Navy's Elwood Ammunition Depot and read:

NO ADMITTANCE
EXCEPT ON DUTY

It was, of course, nailed to the door of the Boulevard Inn.

Another remembered event was when the well diggers came with their horse and drilling gear. The horse walked in a circle around the well site, driving the drill that found a bountiful supply of cool, pure water at 32 feet. The well was capped and a pump installed. On that day the children and their mother celebrated the end to child servitude. For three summers the children had trudged to the Erland pump house and back, a round trip of a quarter-mile, each carrying one or two buckets of water. For this purpose there was an assortment of buckets: 12-quart for John, 8-quart for Helga and 4-quart for Roald, the youngest. On those rare days when Marie needed a wash tub full for washing clothes and another for rinsing them, the children made numerous trips.

Marie often made doughnuts; small, crispy circles of heavenly eating. When the children harvested native huckleberries, Marie would bake a pie. There were the small true wild blackberries that gave pies a mouth-watering flavor and from the Erland's pasture, a few cups of tiny wild strawberries eaten with thick cream and a dab of sugar.

John built a simple but effective arched gateway for the beach entrance to the property. Gunnar always referred to the cabin as *Lundar*, country Norwegian for "groves" and the plural of Lund. So Helga, using small branches, put the name at the top of the gateway to Gunnar's delight, but explaining that unusual name to non-Norwegians was often a problem for the children.

When company came from Seattle, Marie would have the children strew huckleberry greens and small fir branches by the entrances to the cabin porch to "make things look festive."

Above the cabin a trail led through the firs to the orchard, Gunnar's special place. There he planted fruit trees, three rows of Himalaya blackberries and an area of currents and gooseberries. Clad in khakis, his customary beach clothing, Gunnar spent happy hours working there. Nearer the cabin was the woodpile and sawbuck. Every weekend morning he would trundle the wooden wheelbarrow down to the beach, hunt for the bounty the tide had brought in, and bring back bark and wood for the cookstove that also provided the only heat for the cabin. He was never to be convinced that driftwood and bark, which had soaked in the salt water, would rust out the stove. Consequently, the Lunds purchased a new (but pre-owned and used) kitchen range every few years.

None of the children can remember a summer weekend when Gunnar failed to saw and split some firewood. It was work he loved.

During summer months Gunnar arrived from Seattle on the late boat on Friday afternoon, carrying a valise containing extra pipe tobacco, an envelope of proofs to read and other homework, plus any mail for Marie. The valise also contained the main course for Friday evening dinner, quite often thick sausages, always some fresh fruit and invariably something special for the children such as Charms or other candy. He would leave for Seattle again on the six o'clock boat on Monday mornings, refreshed, rested, ready for another week of bachelor living in Seattle. Unlike his city neighbors, Gunnar never took a one or two-week vacation.

Since there was no telephone service at Erland, Gunnar would take to Seattle a grocery list he phoned in to Helgesen's, the Norwegian grocery store. The groceries were delivered in stout, nailed-shut wooden boxes to the Tuesday afternoon "freight run" of the *F. G. Reeve*. On that day every week the *Reeve* would makes its only trip to Elwood, two miles south of Erland Point, and stop at the Erland dock to unload groceries and any other things that were being freighted out from Seattle.

Two lots south of Lundar was what the children called "the old Indian Church." It had been a Catholic mission for the local Indians of the Chico tribe. In much earlier days a Catholic priest came by motorboat once or twice a month to hear confessions and hold mass. Services were announced by the bell hanging in the belfry. Some years after the Lunds had built their cabin, new owners rebuilt the abandoned mission building into a house. A quarter mile past the old mission was a badly overgrown Indian orchard with Damson plums and old apple trees, plus a sprawling hedge of evergreen blackberries.

Gradually the Erlands sold off their lots and the Lunds had neighbors. Magnus Jordan was the first of these. A retired lighthouse keeper, he built a snug house for himself, cleared his land and planted grapes. The vineyard had two purposes: the sale of Concord grapes to people wishing to make juice or jelly, and conversion of other varieties into wine for Jordan's personal consumption. He was a friend to all the children. When the Fourth of July came around he always gave the children five dollars to buy fireworks at the Chico store for the big event on the Point. For days the children combed the beaches to find wood for a huge bonfire to be touched off just before dark on the Fourth.

Two nights before one Fourth of July celebration Jordan, possibly slightly affected by some of his wine, went to his front porch with a rocket in his hand, lit it, and remembered too late that a rocket must always be put in a firing trough. He came to the big fire a few nights later with his hand greatly swollen and swathed in a crude bandage. We all thought Jordan was a run-of-the mill American until one night, again feeling his wine, he went to his front porch and shouted in Norwegian, "My name is not Jordan but *Jordal.*"

Pastor Stub and his family rented the cabin just south of the Lund cabin for two summers. Stub, whose name was pronounced "Stewb," was minister of the (Norwegian) Immanuel Lutheran Church in Seattle, where Marie was a member. Victoria, the minister's wife, was a close friend of Marie's, and the children Gerhard and Sylvia were close companions of the two older Lund children. Helga would sketch out plays and she and Sylvia would stage them on the Stub front porch for a noisily appreciative young audience.

Except for the summers when she was at Erland, Marie frequently went to services at Immanuel Lutheran, where she was a member. Gunnar's attendance was limited to Easter and, just possibly, Christmas. He was a quietly self-proclaimed agnostic. Yet he and Pastor Stub were great friends and Gunnar enjoyed his company.

The major daytime occupation for the children at Erland was swimming, and the finely pebbled beach of the point was the gathering place for water fun and sunning. At the Lund household the after-swimming food of choice was a large slab of Swedish rye crispbread, lathered with butter and consumed during toweling and dressing.

Eventually when a road was built to Erland the sale of property mushroomed and dozens of families attended the nightly fires on the point with marshmallow and hot dog treats. With the road came electricity and Roald at 15 wired the cabin. Gunnar, who had zero aptitude in things mechanical or electrical, quietly confided to Marie "The boy is very, very bright. I think he may turn out to be something after all."

John spent one summer working at Paradise Inn on Mt. Rainer, saving his money for what he needed most in life, an Evinrude outboard motor that would make him the official though uncompensated ferryboat skipper. With the advent of the road, most people came with their cars on the Bremerton ferry and drove to Erland. This change greatly reduced travel to Erland on the *F. G. Reeve* , which now only made the trip across the bay to the Point for a minimum of four fares. The *Reeve* would toot twice after the standard single toot for Tracyton. This signal informed John there was one or more passengers for Erland. John and a friend would hustle the motor from the dockhouse to the shore, mount it on the rowboat and struggle through the ordeal of starting the one cylinder motor. Under ideal conditions it might start with a pull or two. Sometimes it might take half an hour or more.

One Sunday Marie's Norwegian Hospital Association had its annual picnic at Erland, with heavy participation by the Erland family and neighbors. A bountiful clam chowder and salad lunch was served. One of the events was a swimming party that almost ended in tragedy. A Mrs. Dahl had ignored warnings against swimming on the north side of the point because of the heavy tide running there. The strong current began to carry her out. In a panic she began going under. Helga and Sylvia swam to the rescue and held her up until a rowboat could be launched to bring Mrs. Dahl back to shore.

Erland was a constant stream of adventure for the children. There were hikes led by Mary Erland to Kitsap and Wildcat lakes for swimming parties. There were small group hikes and rowboat trips by the children to the Chico or the Elwood stores for bottles of pop and minor groceries for the families. The Chico hike was a favorite for it took them through the farms at the end of what the children called "mud bay" and across Chico Creek, an alluring area for exploration. In the fall salmon would come thrashing up the shallow creek to spawn. There were haying parties on the Erland farm. For Roald and his age group, sailing in the heavy V-bottom rowboats with homemade sails, masts and gear provided hours of pleasant adventure. There was fishing: from the dock for perch, across the bay at Rocky Point for cod, and trolling for trout closer to home.

Helga often staged plays and other entertainment on neighbors' porches. Almost every evening there were bonfires with story telling, group singing, and games.

On many weekends in the fall and spring Gunnar took Roald along to Bremerton by ferry, then by stage to a drop-off point two miles from Erland Point. They trudged in to the cabin and had a simple dinner before Gunnar tackled his homework under the kerosene mantle lamp in the days before electricity. On many evenings they walked up to the Erland house where Gunnar and Knut talked and smoked. One especially memorable occasion occurred when the Sunday bus had engine trouble and missed the ferry to Seattle at Bremerton. Gunnar had a committee meeting he had to attend, and Roald talked him into taking the Air Ferry, a ponderous big Sikorski flying boat. For Gunnar it was a white-knuckle trip. He never tired of telling people that one week later the Air Ferry went down with two casualties.

The cabin was a continuing source of joy to the whole family, but their affection for it was shattered one fall weekend when Gunnar had gone alone out to the cabin. On Sunday afternoon in Seattle Roald was listening to radio news when he shouted for Marie and Helga. Six people had been murdered in the Fleider home, just a few hundred feet from the Lund cabin. There had been a party Saturday night. One of the dead was identified as Magnus Jordan, two more were the Fleiders, three others were unidentified. Gunnar was not due home for several hours. Marie, Helga and Roald waited, hardly daring to talk, but Gunnar came home on time, completely unaware of what had occurred just three houses away while he slept Saturday night in the cabin.

Six months later the Lunds found a buyer for the property. It was, for all the family, the end of the Erland adventure. They closed up the cabin for the last time, taking a few possessions before turning the simple passkey over to the new owner.

Twenty years later, Roald was driven by the need to see Erland again. He and his wife Edna took the Bremerton ferry and drove out to the Point, It was to be Edna's first exposure to the summer retreat that she had heard of so many times. For Roald the changes were crushing. Erland Point had become a bedroom community for Bremerton workers and their families. The old Lund cabin was gone. Their former property now held three houses, and on the finely graveled point itself a house had been built. The dock was falling apart.

When the couple walked down the beach from the point and saw what used to be Lundar, Roald turned back saying, "I can't take this. Let's go to the car and get out of here."

Without his seeing it Edna, behind him, picked up three

fairly large stones from the beach and put them in the generous bag she had been carrying. Back at their home on Bull Mountain near Tigard, she carefully placed the three stones at the corner of the Portuguese laurel hedge they had just planted. They are still there today: a last reminder of the cabin on Puget Sound, so beloved by the whole Lund family and especially by Gunnar, for whom it fulfilled the natural need of a city dweller from Norway for his own *hytte*.

Chapter 8

THE TWENTIES

In the issue of May 13, 1920, Gunnar issued a challenge and started what he hoped would be a short-range campaign. He urged the Norwegian organizations of Seattle to set a goal for a combined Seventeenth of May festival with net proceeds designated to build the Norwegian Hospital in Seattle. There are, he insisted "too many Seventeenth of May festivals competing with each other. The Norwegian Hospital Association has been striving for a long time and has collected a substantial building fund." He pointed out that a Norwegian Hospital would be a fitting memorial to the Norwegian-American immigrants. The same issue held advertisements for seven separate Seventeenth of May festivals in Seattle.

He repeated the challenge in the issue of May 20. "It is time we had a united celebration. There are too many now, with too few attending each of them." He was to repeat the challenge year after year until he achieved the unity he saw as needed.

Immediately after the 1920 Seventeenth of May festival in Norway Hall, *Washington Posten* congratulated the local Sons and Daughters of Norway lodges for their successful effort in bringing back "the good old Constitution Day celebration to Seattle." The main speaker was Pastor R. E.

Bergersen whom Gunnar praised "for his deeply felt handling of the important question: could one be a good American and still hold strong interest in the land he had left?" The pastor strongly regretted the fanatic spirit that had been so prevalent during the war years. He admitted his own "guilt" in being interested in his old fatherland, its welfare, its language and his memories. Was that incompatible with his duties to America? Was he being disloyal? He did not think so.

He was proud of what Norway's great men had accomplished, but proudest of all of the accomplishments the common Norwegian immigrants had achieved in this country. The speaker defended the Norwegian Lutheran Church in America for wanting to change to the English language because the immigrants' children were not learning Norwegian and the church had to be realistic. "But our people could just as well try to tear their hearts out as to tear the Norwegian out of their hearts."

Professor E. J. Vickner of the Scandinavian department at the University of Washington, speaking in English and Swedish, brought greetings from the Swedish people for the immense work the Norwegians had done to advance freedom and social reform. They, he declared, had shown Sweden the way.

In an October issue the paper told of the death of Julius Sunde, age 63. He had been *Washington Posten's* print shop foreman from the very first issue in 1889.

The November 5th issue reported that Knut Hamsun, Norway's most famous living author, had been awarded the Nobel Prize for literature for 1920. The first shipment of his latest book, *Markens Grøde*, translated into English as "Growth of the Soil" sold out in a few days at Lowman & Hanford Co. in Seattle.

In January of 1921 the paper reprinted in part an article from the *Atlantic Monthly*, reporting that most of the third-class passengers on a Norwegian ship (unidentified but probably of the Norwegian-America Line) were Norwegians, Swedes and Danes returning permanently to their home countries after years in America. Many said they were going home to a freer, better country. The paper's headline on the story was "What is the Reason?" It could not provide an answer.

In July the newspaper reported that Roald Amundsen was enroute on the *SS Victoria* from Nome. His ship, the *Maud*, had lost its propeller so it was coming to Seattle under sail and was not expected to reach Seattle until October. The Norwegian parliament had assured funds for repair and outfitting for Amundsen's next polar voyage.

When the *Maud* arrived it tied up at the Sunde & d'Evers dock and the Lund family joined the welcoming throng. Later that week Amundsen and members of his crew came to the Lund home for dinner. On their way, Amundsen learned that most of his party had eaten dinner aboard ship, fearing that "American women didn't know how to cook and there wouldn't be enough food for us, anyway."

Amundsen was angry and told them they would be in trouble if they didn't clean their plates. He need not have worried. They all had second helpings of the typical Norwegian dinner Marie served. At the dinner, Amundsen met his namesake, Roald Lund, who was then nine years old. "I hope," Amundsen told Marie, "that he gives you less trouble than I gave my mother."

Amundsen was jovial, enormously impressive, and both Gunnar and Marie considered his visit the high mark of their year.

That year the Dovre railway was opened, cutting three hours off the trip from Oslo to Trondheim. A few months later Trondheim erected its heroic statue of Olav Trygvason in the Town Square. Trygvason was the Viking king who died in the year 1000 and had made the first effort to Christianize Norway.

Gunnar used his editorial column to stand up for the right of Japanese, Polish and Italian language newspapers to be critical of our government's immigration laws. He singled out U.S. Congressman Albert Johnson who had in a speech urged "wiping out of all foreign-language papers." This Gunnar called a result of some of these papers objecting to the new immigration policies of the U.S.

Gunnar's editorial declared Johnson's proper role was "not to bait the foreign born citizens but to set an example of fair and equal treatment to all our citizens. Foreign-language newspapers have just as legitimate a field as their English-language contemporaries and the Constitution of the U.S. protects them in all their lawful activities. Our immigrant press, according to recent statistics, is just as truly loyal to America as the press in the English language – if anything, more so."

Defending the immigrant, President Coolidge was quoted as saying, "The best way for us who wish all our inhabitants to be single minded in their Americanism, is for us to bestow upon each one that confidence and fellowship which is due all Americans. If we want to get the hysteria out of our country we can best begin by taking it out of our minds."

But despite pro-immigrant rhetoric, in 1921 the door that had been so open and welcoming to foreigners was now beginning to close. With that closing the immigrant epic was to end. Together with the impact of the depression of the thirties, the inevitable casualties would include major members of the Norwegian-language press. *Skandinaven* in Chicago would cease publishing its daily edition. In 1941 it would stop its weekly. In 1932 *Minneapolis Tidende* would fold its daily and quit totally in 1935. With the death of Waldemar Ager in 1941 his publication *Reform* in Eau Claire, Wisconsin, suspended publication.

For *Washingon Posten* the twenties would see its circulation peak at 15,000 and then begin to fall. Across America editors of all remaining Norwegian newspapers had reason to be concerned as to the survival of their own papers.

They commented on the loss of the two papers and they were especially touched by Ager's death. The noted linguist and scholar Einar Haugen wrote a literary biography of Ager and entitled it "Immigrant Idealist." Haugen cited Ager's three goals: to eliminate alcohol use from American life, to preserve the Norwegian language among the descendants of the immigrants, and to inspire a growing, vibrant Norwegian-American literature widely read by Norwegian-Americans. Ager failed in all three. He was indeed the great Norwegian-American idealist.

The Nobel Peace Prize for 1922, voted by a special committee of the Norwegian *Storting* (parliament), went to Fridtjof Nansen for his work in assisting displaced persons and war prisoners of the World War. Nansen, a world famous explorer, oceanographer, statesman, diplomat and humanitarian created a special document known as the "Nansen passport" which enabled such persons to return to their native countries.

A crushing blow came to many Seattle Scandinavians with the closure of the Scandinavian-American Bank. It was declared insolvent and the winding up of its affairs was in the hands of the State Supervisor of Banking.

At the end of 1922 the Norwegian Hospital Association purchased the Lakeside Hospital in the north end of Seattle and *Washington Posten* ran a large picture of the old mansion.

Gertrude Anderson was chosen to be the general manager. The dedication was on Sunday, January 7, 1923.

Again, in its edition following May 17, *Washington Posten* criticized the Seattle Norwegian-Americans for their failure to unite in one combined celebration. It pointed to the fact that the Norwegian Hospital Association had again filled the Masonic Temple to provide the biggest fete and that "it is imperative that we Norwegians show what we can do together."

The pulling power of the Norwegian Hospital Association's festivals was no accident. Marie Lund, its long-time president, was a dynamo of ideas and action. She brought together the brightest and hardest working women in the community to create and stage impressive events that attracted increasing crowds. An example was the staging of the historic "Bridal Voyage in Hardanger," an enactment of the famous Norwegian painting. Thousands came to watch from the shore of Lake Washington as the bridal party landed, with a fiddler in the bow of the boat. The beautifully presented event earned great publicity in the daily papers, netted $1,500 for the sponsoring Norwegian Hospital Association, and was pronounced "highly successful."

During October the great Norwegian author Johan Boyer (*"The Last Viking"* was his best known work) was in Seattle on a speaking tour of the U.S. He also appeared in Great Falls, Spokane, Silvana, Everett, Poulsbo, Tacoma, Hoquiam, Portland, Oakland, San Francisco and Los Angeles.

A *Bergen Aftenblad* journalist touring America reported that the University of Washington had five professors in its fisheries department and asked, "When will the University of Oslo have one?"

In February 1925, one hundred years of Norwegian immigration to the United States was observed. The tiny sloop *Restauration* had left Stavanger for New York in 1825 with 52 aboard. It arrived with 53 passengers; the youngest was born during the long voyage. The centennial was observed across America and Seattle staged one of the biggest celebrations at the University of Washington Stadium. Marie was deeply involved in the planning and execution.

Washington Posten announced the opening of its office bookstore of Norwegian language books including Undset, Falkberget, Bjørnson and many other Norwegian authors including the most popular current writers.

The paper also reported in July 1924 that in Norway popular Crown Prince Olav celebrated his 21st birthday, and the Norwegian flag was flown throughout the country.

The name of O. J. Ejde, the assistant editor, disappeared from the masthead of *Washington Posten* for several years. He did write a few lengthy articles about dory fishing from the halibut schooner *Scandia* off Kodiak Island and 300 miles from shore in the Gulf of Alaska.

The biggest news from Norway in 1925 came on January first, when the name of the capital city Kristiania (spelled Christiania in English) was officially changed to Oslo.

Gunnar had been editor and publisher of *Washington Posten* for 20 years by November 1925. He had shaped *Washington Posten* into an effective, well-edited newspaper, and had increased the subscription list many times over. The experience in these years had also shaped Gunnar. Much of the change in him was accomplished through a process of unconscious adaptation to the many pressures that affect any editor. He learned through handling problems to his best ability. He once commented that he frequently felt his work was less than fully professional and that education for the editor job was something he should have had, but that self-critical attitude goaded him to think out solutions to problems and in so doing he increased his skill.

The constant short deadlines and the insatiable appetite of the linotype operator for more copy forced Gunnar to be disciplined and to develop the ability to work faster. At the end of each weekly production cycle he re-read the paper that was the result of his work. He apparently felt he must not try to escape that task, and that exercise helped him improve his writing, his selection of news priorities, and his reaching out for new or better sources of news.

He had come far in those twenty years and farther yet in the thirty-six years since he first came to the United States. In those first years he shoveled gravel, worked on a track-laying gang, fed a church furnace, helped load lumber onto ships and worked in manual labor jobs that were the only option for an immigrant with little English. Granted he did step up to better jobs in time, but the move to becoming editor and publisher of *Washington Posten* was a quantum leap. He made the leap with no training in related work and fought his way to success by sheer perseverance.

He never lost sight of one self-imposed maxim: the news comes first. This is where he placed his emphasis. Accordingly, editorial comment was reserved for urgent issues. There were plenty of urgent issues. He was never hesitant about defending the rights of the foreign-born or advocating a cause that would benefit Norwegian-Americans. He frequently wrote about the meaning of American holidays or great Americans because he had an innate sense of obligation to his adopted country. He remained a Norwegian who had become a practicing American citizen. He believed that the Norwegians had much to contribute to their new country – the whole bundle of characteristics, ethics, morals, eagerness to work and devotion to freedom and democracy that he so thoroughly represented in his own life.

Looking back, it can be said that Gunnar gave *Washington Posten* steady, strong, intelligent leadership. Conversely, *Washington Posten* gave Gunnar the big opportunity of his working life, that the task of editing and publishing a newspaper made a great change in Gunnar. It was his great good fortune to be given that opportunity and to have a wife like Marie who had urged him to take the opportunity and had never stopped supporting him.

In March 1925 *Washington Posten* repeated its urgent plea for a united Seventeenth of May festival with all profits to go to the Norwegian Hospital Association. In the same issue the Norwegian Hospital Association made a "proposal to the Norwegian people" undersigned by a hundred prominent Norwegian-Americans and all 36 Association members. The proposal was that the Norwegian-Americans of the area unite to finance and build a new modern hospital, illustrated by an architect's drawing of the proposed building.

During 1927 Gunnar and Marie saw their eldest son John off to his year as a graduate student at the University in Oslo. John wrote a short series of articles for the paper which appeared in a page one position in the Norwegian language but it appears the articles were translated by his father from John's English originals, for John's Norwegian was hardly that good.

In the March 4 issue, there was news of the wreck of the halibut schooner *Scandia*, which had hit a rock and sunk. All members of the crew were saved, including Capt. Olav O. Hvatum and O. L. Ejde, who would return to his position as assistant editor at *Washington Posten* within a few months. The *Scandia* had been under charter to the International Fisheries Commision during the past year to research life and habits of halibut.

Roald Amundsen visited Seattle in April speaking on his successful flight over the North Pole. Gunnar was delighted to see him again. *Washington Posten* reported enthusiastically on Amundsen's public address.

Also in 1927 Gunnar Lund left for Norway as one of twelve American journalists invited to the country as guests of the government. There were three other Norwegian-American newspapermen in the party, A. N. Rygg of *Nordisk Tidende,* Brooklyn; Christian Prestgaard of *Decorah Posten,* Decorah, Iowa; and John A. Anderson of *Skandinaven,* Chicago. Rygg and Lund, both from Stavanger originally, had lived in the same boarding house in Chicago many years before. They recalled they had paid $12 a month for a large living room and bedroom and $3 a week for meals.

The Norway excursion included a trip on the *Stavangerfjord* to North Cape and Hammerfest, and passage to and from Brooklyn on the *Bergensfjord.* Both ships were provided by the Norwegian America Line.

Gunnar wrote articles for *Washington Posten* each week. In one he told of his great pleasure on seeing Telemark again. He recalled hiking through the area from his native Stavanger on the way to his studies at the University in Kristiania, pack on his back, staff in hand, and sleeping "out" nights. Each of these trips took him several weeks or more and his costs for a trip were as low as 30 to 40 kroner for food.

Gunnar did not mention in his many articles his audience with King Haakon, nor did he mention thanking the king for the award he had received on December 5, 1926 in recognition of his years of service to the Norwegian-Americans of the West, his election to the Order of St. Olav as knight, first class.

Gunnar purchased his suits from P. O. Wold who not only had his tailoring establishment in the same building

The editor in the "sporty" checkered suit that he was forced to wear for his audience with King Haakon — Seattle 1927.

with *Washington Posten* but also advertised regularly in the paper. As a change from his usual conservative wear, and against the advice of Wold, Gunnar had chosen a sporty checkered wool on his last visit to Wold and this he wore as a travel garment on the Norway trip.

Unfortunately, his main baggage was late in arriving in Oslo, so Gunnar was forced to wear the inappropriate and less than conservative checkered suit for his audience with the king. He was pleased that King Haakon brushed aside his apologies with a smile and said he only wished he could dress that informally.

In 1928 there were four separate Seventeenth of May festivals in Seattle. Again, Gunnar's editorial called for a united celebration. Just a few weeks later Leif Erikson Lodge, Sons of Norway, took the first step toward a combined festival in the huge new Seattle Civic Auditorium. A committee was named by the lodge to contact all Norwegian organizations in the city to plan for the united 1929 celebration.

During this time Helga Lund filled in at the *Washington Posten* office on occasion, doing such odd jobs as writing individual notes to subscribers whose payments were long overdue. At dinner one night Gunnar reported he had received a check for eight years from a reader who had received such a note from Helga. "Gunnar," Marie protested, "Do you let the paper run that long to someone who doesn't pay?" Gunnar answered, "He is a countryman, Marie. I knew that when he had the cash money he would pay up,"

In June of 1928 it was reported that the dirigible *Italia*, commanded by Gen. Umberto Nobile, was assumed lost in its attempted flight from Svalbard to reach the North Pole. Roald Amundsen quickly organized a rescue mission and took off in a floatplane to hunt for the missing Italians. Amundsen did not return, but Nobile found his way back. Norway and Norwegian-Americans went into mourning for the heroic Amundsen. Memorial services were scheduled in Norway and also in Seattle and many other American cities.

On a cold wet night in the fall of 1928 there were some hours of frantic concern in the Lund household. Gunnar always walked home from the office invariably arriving a few minutes before six each evening. On that night he failed to appear. By seven o'clock Marie had called her son John in Camas, Washington, to report the problem. He suggested calling the police and said he would start for Seattle in a matter of minutes, a drive taking at least six hours.

A few minutes before eight the doorbell rang. It was a "Good Samaritan" who found Gunnar lying barely conscious in doorway of a closed store, bleeding from a head wound and abrasions on his right side. Those were the days of house calls, and Dr. Loe came within twenty minutes.

Walking home in the dark Gunnar had been struck by a hit-and-run driver and had suffered a serious concussion. It was many weeks before he was allowed to get back to his office.

In December the Nobel Prize for literature was awarded to Sigrid Undset, author of *Kristin Lavransdatter*.

The Seattle Repertory Playhouse performed Ibsen's *Wild Duck* in April 1929. Everett Armstrong, the *Post-Intelligencer's* dean of Seattle critics, wrote "Helga Lund was the talented young actress who so understandingly portrayed little Hedvig, possibly the most moving role in all dramatic literature. Herself of Norwegian descent, Miss Lund brings both intelligence and scenic talents to her interpretation of the young victim of idealism in Ibsen's masterwork. She was on the opening evening an outstanding member among the players."

Gunnar, not one moved to praise any member of his family in *Washington Posten*, simply quoted the review. He was visibly touched by its warmth. However, some months later the paper carried a detailed review and analysis of the Repertory's presentation of the *Master Builder*, praising the players including Helga Lund for her role of Hilde.

Finally, Gunnar's long crusade for a united Seventeenth of May celebration bore fruit. The Sons and Daughters of Norway lodges, the Norwegian Hospital Association, and the Norwegian Male Chorus drew attendance of 4,000 to the Civic Auditorium. Editorially, Gunnar expressed "a hearty 'thank you' we all owe the organizations for good collaboration. We are all proud and grateful for what this has achieved for us all."

"Wireless" news from Norway to the Norwegian-American press was instituted the first week of August in 1929, ending the long time gap between events in Norway and news in the Norwegian-language press. Formerly, the papers here received exchange papers from Norway by mail, ensuring a time delay of up to three weeks or more.

One of Norway's and the world's bright stars, Sonja Henie, came to New York to perform in the January 6 carnival of the National Figure Skating Association in Madison Square Garden.

Seattle had its first opportunity to hear baritone August Werner in concert with the Norwegian Male Chorus in early December. He would return to the city a number of times and eventually join the University of Washington music department. Werner, a talented artist and sculptor as well as a first rank singer, became a highly appreciated fixture of Sangerfests for years.

Also in early December, O. L. Ejde started a three part series "The Halibut Fleet and Its Men" in *Washington Posten*.

Chapter 9

THE THIRTIES

A major *Washington Posten* story of 1930 came in the issue of February 21. It was a follow-up story on the polar flight of the Italian General Umberto Nobile in the dirigible *Italia*. The story described Nobile's polar flight as one of the most misfortune-plagued polar expeditions in history. It cost seventeen lives, eight of Nobile's group and nine in Amundsen's failed attempt to rescue Nobile's group. Among the nine was the greatest polar explorer of our time, Roald Amundsen, who had flown a floatplane on the tragic rescue mission. A float, believed to have been from Amundsen's plane, was later found near Tromsø. Nobile himself survived, and lived to be harshly criticized by his own Italian government.

A stone monument or *bautestein* for Amundsen was unveiled in San Francisco's Golden Gate Park beside his original Northwest Passage ship, the *Gjøa*.

Another well-known Norwegian explorer died on May 13, Fridtjof Nansen, who had gained international fame for his famine relief and other humanitarian work after World War I.

July 29, 1930 was a major festival day in Norway. It was in observance of the death of Saint Olav, Olav Haraldsson, in the battle of Stiklestad one thousand years before. He was the first effective king of all Norway and became the country's patron saint. He was noted for his intensive efforts to introduce Christianity in Norway.

So major an event was this coming celebration that Gunnar decided *Washington Posten* needed more than just dispatches from Norway. The paper needed its own correspondent to see, to feel and to report the national observance and especially details of the observance in the Trondelag area. Who could be better than someone with Trondelag roots? This was not a surprise assignment for Marie Lund — it was her long-time dream and hope to pay one more visit to the land of her birth. She took her daughter Helga who typed in Norwegian all Marie's many penciled articles. One of the high points in their experience in Norway was an audience with King Haakon, which gave Marie the opportunity to thank him for the Olav medallion she had received for her services to the Norwegian immigrants.

Marie's reports were featured on the front pages of *Washington Posten*. The series carried the standing title *Ferden til Fedreland* (Voyage to (My) Native Land). The articles also became a book, published by *Washington Posten* as *Dette er Norge* (This is Norway). And indeed it was, all 252 pages. It covered the festivities at Stiklestad and at the oldest cathedral in Scandinavia, the *Trondheim Domkirke*. The articles began with boarding of the Norwegian America Line *Stavangerfjord* at Brooklyn in early May and ended with the homebound trip on the *Bergensfjord* with arrival in Seattle in mid-September of 1930.

While her initial focus was on the millennial festivities, the articles also included Marie's travels all over the country and her visits to Vardø, the city or her birth in far northern Norway. There she hoped to find some trace of her parents, but was not successful. She also visited and wrote about the valley of her father's people, Oppdal; Grieg's city, Bergen; the Seventeenth of May in Oslo; Gunnar's city Stavanger; and her sister's home at Brekstad on Ørlandet. Her articles gave special emphasis to the outstanding women of Norway and their contribution to the progress and welfare of that country.

Marie came home to a troubled situation in the Norwegian Hospital Association. There was a heavy mortgage payment due on the building and insufficient funds to meet it. There was also a major depression that made fund-raising impossible.

The money crunch had also hit *Washington Posten*. Advertising revenue was dropping markedly and circulation declined sharply as loyal old subscribers felt the depression pinch and cancelled their subscriptions or delayed payment. Potential new subscribers felt that groceries were more important than getting a Norwegian-American newspaper.

Belts were tightened at the paper. Budgets were reduced; corners were cut. But Gunnar kept the newspaper running, even if it meant that his personal income suffered heavily. He knew that across the country many foreign-language newspapers, including Norwegian papers, were giving up. He was determined that *Washington Posten* would weather the bad times, no matter what. Now, it was really a time of wear out, make do, do without.

A month later it was time to report the twenty-fifth anniversary of King Haakon and the wholehearted observance Norway gave to that event.

The Seattle Repertory Playhouse opened its splendid performance of Ibsen's *Peer Gynt* with a cast of 60 – one of whom was Helga Lund, who played the lead role of Solveig.

In March 1931 the Seattle Ski Club held its first annual ski jumping event at Summit in the Cascades. And the April 4 edition of *Washington Posten* had O. L. Ejde listed again as assistant editor. He would remain with the paper until he retired in 1964. Now he was back in harness, much to the relief and pleasure of Gunnar who needed Ejde's competent help.

A famous Norwegian-American's death became page one news in the edition of April 3 – Knute Rockne.

The impact of the depression was felt by the united 17th of May celebration in Seattle. Attendance dropped 20% to 4,000.

Washington Posten extended birthday congratulations to N. A. Grevstad, editor of *Skandinaven* in Chicago. He was eighty years old and still the editor.

In October Gunnar had personal reasons to mourn the death of Frank Oleson. He had founded *Washington Posten* in 1889 and was the man who convinced Gunnar to purchase the paper and be its editor and publisher. Gunnar characterized Oleson as having played a leading role among Norwegian-Americans in Seattle. He had come to this country at the age of 20. In the last days before his death at 70 Oleson spoke of his great happiness from having participated in and written of the life and work of Norwegian-Americans in Seattle and the West.

In Northfield, Minnesota, Ole Edvart Rølvaag died, author of the *Giants in the Earth* trilogy, *The Boat of Longing*, and other novels. He was, Gunnar commented editorially, proof of the truth that is part of our Norwegian heritage, that a man must be his best and also a useful citizen. Rølvaag was a professor at St. Olaf College and wrote his sagas of prairie life in Norwegian. They were first published in Norway, then translated and published in many countries, especially the United States, England and Germany. In his youth he was a fisherman in the Nordland area, he immigrated to the United States where he became an honored teacher and author.

In January, 1932 Gunnar was happy to report that E. J.

Vickner, the Swedish-born head of the University of Washington Scandinavian department, was presented with the Order of St. Olav; Consul for Norway Thos. E. Kolderup made the presentation on behalf of King Haakon.

In this worst year of the local depression, the united Seventeenth of May celebration retreated from the Civic Auditorium to the Masonic Temple. With admission pared to 50 cents, there was a full house of over 2,000 attendees, just twenty percent of the biggest year on record. *Washington Posten* regretfully cut its weekly size from eight pages down to six pages as a cost-saving measure.

Important events of the year included August Werner taking up residence in Seattle. From his post at the University of Washington he added significantly to the cultural and artistic resources of the Norwegian community.

Another event of importance was the founding of the Norwegian Commercial Club. Gunnar, a charter member, welcomed it as another worthwhile effort.

In December Norway Hall saw the centennial celebration of the birth of Bjørnstjerne Bjørnson. It was one of many observances all over the United States. In the same month Einar Beyer became Norwegian Consul, a move necessitated by the death of Consul Kolderup.

To stress its importance to advertisers as well as the public, *Washington Posten* began to run banner lines above the logotype name of the paper. They read: "A Norwegian Newspaper With The Largest Circulation Of Any Foreign Language Newspaper In The Pacific Northwest."

1933 saw another reduction in advertising lineage, a punishing drain on *Washington Posten's* revenues. With the depression still raging, many subscribers were unable to spend $1.50 for the annual renewal, but the paper continued to come to them, even if they owed for five years, especially if they were subscribers who had received the paper for ten years or more.

Ski news became big, with jumps in Spokane, a championship jump of the Seattle Ski Club at Snoqualmie Summit and in March a jump of the Portland Ski Club at Timberline.

In late March *Washington Posten* announced the discontinuation of two major Norwegian newspapers in the Midwest. Under the heading "SOS" the editorial asked "what will happen to our organization without the help of the Norwegian press?" In the next issue a letter from B. O. Clausen of Seattle appeared, expressing his dismay on hearing of the loss of the two papers and urgently advising readers to support the Norwegian-language press.

Mirroring the continuing depression, Norway cancelled the pending visit of Crown Prince Olav and Princess Martha. The explanation: poor timing in view of economic conditions in both the U.S. and Norway.

Another casualty of the depression, the Norwegian Hospital in Seattle quietly closed its doors, unable to make its mortgage payments. The Norwegian Hospital Association continued into the next century, supporting such activities as the Norse Home (a retirement home) which would later be built in Seattle. The closing of the Hospital was a shattering blow to Marie Lund, president of the Association. She had devoted years of work to the cause. It was equally hard on the many other members of the Association who had labored to make the dream of a hospital a living reality.

In 1933 the Seventeenth of May joint committee in Seattle prudently held their festival in a much smaller hall than the Civic Auditorium which they had filled in better times. They filled the Masonic Temple at a reduced fee of 35 cents with children free. Consul Einar Beyer was the speaker and August

Werner was soloist with the Norwegian Male Chorus.

Indicating a trend that would eventually sweep through the lodges of the Sons and Daughters of Norway, the headquarters in Minneapolis approved use of the English language in organization of the Knute Rockne Lodge in Seattle. It was a lodge of young people, predominantly second generation; it was not the first lodge to use the English language exclusively. Commenting editorially, Gunnar welcomed the new lodge, and admitted, "We have failed to convince our youth that those who own two languages are far richer than those who own only one."

He did not blame the immigrants for not teaching their children to speak Norwegian. That he could hardly do, for in their own home he and Marie spoke English exclusively. They never spoke Norwegian to their children. It was Gunnar's position that he wanted to be sure "there was no barrier for the children becoming good Americans." Professionally, he was editor of a Norwegian-language newspaper, and he editorialized on the need to preserve the language. He agreed fully with the authors and devoted Norwegians, Waldemar Ager and O. E. Rølvaag, that allowing the Norwegian language to die in America would be tragic. Ager insisted: "If the language falls into disuse, then the interest in things Norwegian also dies."

Gunnar and Marie had both struggled to become totally at home in the English language. They both spoke English fluently with hardly a trace of accent. They felt they were helping their children to be at home in America and succeed in this country. As a result, the three children had to struggle on their own to learn Norwegian and never learned to speak or read it fluently. All three regretted that as a major lack in their lives.

Ager's pessimistic prediction was hardly correct, however.

Despite an almost total failure to learn Norwegian, the descendents of the Norwegian immigrants did not forget Norway and things Norwegian. In the future, Scandinavian Airlines System would provide service from Seattle via Copenhagen to Norway and virtually every flight would carry a large number of second, third and fourth generation Norwegian-Americans, making their pilgrimages to the land of their heritage. SAS also provided equally popular service from Minneapolis and from New York. The Sons and Daughters of Norway lodges would also have an increasing percentage of their memberships made up of the descendents of immigrants. Scandinavian import shops would do well not only in metropolitan centers. The popularity of unmistakably Norwegian sweaters, lutefisk and lefse feasts and Norwegian heirlooms and other artifacts in homes would testify that Norway was alive and well in the lives of those who could neither speak nor read the Norwegian language.

By the spring of 1934 there was some hope that the economy was brightening, and the Seattle Seventeenth of May joint committee gambled on holding the annual celebration at the Civic Auditorium again. The gamble paid off with an almost full house. By fall, with the cooperation of all the Scandinavian organizations, a Leif Erickson festival was held in the Civic Auditorium. Dr. Emil Friborg, the Swedish-American minister, was the main speaker. The Norwegian, Swedish and Danish male choruses appeared in one united chorus and they sang numbers from all three countries and also one from Iceland. Rudolf Møller and C. H. Sutherlin directed. Gunnar' editorial commented on the cooperation of all Nordic groups, and called the affair an outstanding success with a total of 5,500 people attending.

Rudolf Møller who directed the Seattle Norwegian Male Chorus and always directed the mass concerts at the

Sangerfests of all affiliated choruses on the Pacific Coast died in February of the next year.

Another well-known Norwegian in the Seattle community George B. Helgesen died in early January of 1934. He had opened his grocery store in 1890. His trucks delivered groceries to Norwegian families all over the city, but towards the end of his life, in the depth of the depression, he delivered only to families living close to his own home on Capitol Hill. He personally carried the bags of groceries by streetcar. In better days it was his happy custom to include a "gift package" – such as a dozen choice oranges – when he received payment for his monthly bill. The Lund family remembered that during summers groceries came to them at Erland Point in great wooden boxes delivered by the Helgesen truck to the *F. G. Reeve* for its weekly Tuesday freight run. They remained Helgesen customers until the store closed after Helgesen's death.

Washington Posten revealed in the spring of 1935 that Norway's famous poet, Herman Wildenvey, had written a prologue for Seattle's Seventeenth of May festival and would personally deliver it. C. Stang-Anderson, vice consul for Norway, would give the welcoming address. Over 4,000 attended the affair.

Milestones of the Seattle Norwegian colony included the retirement of Einar Beyer as Norwegian consul and the death of one of the city's best known Norwegian doctors, Dr. A. O. Loe.

In the 1935 issue of November 22 Gunnar's editorial mentioned that it was now the paper's thirtieth year under the "current publisher and editor." A small box told of an open house at the Lund residence the next Sunday afternoon. Over 150 persons signed the guest book. The *Seattle Times* sent a reporter and photographer to Gunnar's office and an anniversary story appeared with the best picture ever taken

*Gunnar, celebrating his thirtieth year as editor and publisher —
Seattle November 22, 1935. Seattle Times photo.*

of him. It showed him sitting at his rolltop desk, reading a
galley proof, his old bulldog pipe in his mouth. As usual, he
was wearing a high, stiff collar. He seemed to be
concentrating on finding any errors in that proof.

After his visit to America in 1936 Arne Kildahl, head of
Nordmanns Forbundet, the world wide Norse Federation,
declared it was his view that the Norwegian language would
disappear in the United States within one generation unless
immigration for Norwegians was again opened up. Looking
back, it is obvious that this gloomy prediction was, if not
totally correct, at least a fair approximation of the situation.
The second and third generations generally did not speak
Norwegian and only a very small number studied the
language in a few high schools and colleges or in classes

offered by such organizations as the Sons of Norway. In the main the immigrant group was dying off, and they would take the language with them to their graves.

Washington Posten continued almost exclusively Norwegian, though Arthur Jacobson had been writing a newsy English language column about the activities of the second generation.

In April 1936 the paper started featuring a two column weekly series in English by the publisher's youngest son, Roald Lund, who spent most of the year traveling in Norway. The trip was funded by the sale of the Lund's waterfront summer cabin.

Like his sister and brother, he was deeply impressed with Norway. He recalled dynamiting granite from a large field in Oppdal and taking it by sleigh to the "stone dock" which covered more than a hillside acre and ranged in depth from two to fifteen feet. By the very enormity of the pile he recognized that he was adding a token to the labor of generations of Norwegian forbears. It was humbling and satisfying work, and an experience he would never forget.

Upon his return home he wrote a second series on the changing culture of Norway and one describing its "morality of progress." For some months he also wrote a front-page column called "News for Norse-Americans," an English language commentary on current Norwegian news. All his articles were enthusiastic about Norway, and he urged the sons and daughters of immigrants to visit the country and see for themselves how rich their heritage was.

In June 1936 the *Fram*, Fridtjof Nansen's ship designed and used for his "furthest North" voyage of discovery, had its own new home in the great Bygdøy maritime museum complex that would in the future also house the Oseberg Viking ship and Heyerdahl's Kon Tiki. Amundsen also used the *Fram* in his successful expedition to the South Pole.

Seattle was host city for the 1936 Pacific Coast Sangerfest with three gala concerts, one at the Civic Auditorium, one at the University of Washington Meany Hall, and the third at Fortuna Park. August Werner was soloist.

In October the Leif Erickson festival was down in attendance; the all-Scandinavian gathering did not fill the Civic Auditorium. It brought together Norwegians, Swedes, Danes, Finns and Icelandics. *Leikaringen* Norwegian folk dance group and the Norwegian Male Chorus were part of the show. The generous page-one story described the program as nothing but good, including the main speaker, Congressman Knute Hill of Illinois, a graduate of St. Olaf College and a widely known national figure. His parents were from the Rogaland district in Norway.

Famous Norwegian soprano Kirsten Flagstad came to Seattle for a November 1936 concert at Meany Hall, University of Washington. It was a sellout event and, the paper called it "an unforgettable triumph."

Two more Norwegian triumphs occurred in January. Sonja Henie's first film, "One in a Million" came to Seattle, and Norwegian-American skiers won every event in the all-west ski jumping meets.

Back in Norway's *Vestlandet* the herring fishermen were reporting fantastic catches.

The question of the day from a reader of *Washington Posten* was whether Leif Erickson Lodge, Sons of Norway, would appoint a committee to study the idea of building a larger Norway Hall big enough to house "all our organizations and their offices." He feared that some cold water had been thrown on the idea and stated "we rethink the challenge and opportunity since our beautiful little Norway Hall is now outgrown." A new "Norway Center" was finally opened close to what would become the Seattle Center area. Many years later a new hall was built in Ballard which had by that time become Seattle's "little Norway."

Washington Posten's hard-working editor and publisher, Gunnar Lund, suffered a serious stroke early in 1937. A cable was sent to his young son Roald, who started for home, ending his Norway trip. By February Gunnar was reported as recovering and he made it official in a brief item in the paper extending his thanks to the many who had sent their good wishes. In June he was hard at work again, with a long and important article on "the Norwegian language."

Norway, Gunnar wrote, is once more undergoing a major revolution in its language. The previous revolutions took place in 1907 and again in 1917, and now, 20 years since the last big change, there are new rules. He pointed out that *Washington Posten* was the first newspaper in America to keep pace with the past changes because "we thought it necessary that we in America should not be out of step with developments in Norway's language." The purpose of the changes was to bring "country Norwegian" or *nynorsk* and the "national language" or *riksmaal* closer together. This was not just a decision by academics, it was an action by the national parliament.

Changes? Yes, the country language now said goodbye to *kaffistova* (for coffee shop). It now becomes *kaffistua* in the national language as well. Norway was hard at work rewriting dictionaries and school textbooks so the new style could be taught in schools starting in July 1938. Was the average Norwegian city or country dweller happy about the changes? There was no report of general celebration.

In June 1937 the paper printed a picture taken of the flattie sailboat built, owned and piloted by Reidar Gjølme Jr. as it crossed the starting line to win for the second time the *Post-*

Intelligencer cup. His brother was crew.

For the Fourth of July Gunnar wrote his usual fine editorial on the meaning and importance of the occasion, a way of saluting the United States. This was customary for him on such dates as the birthdays of Washington and Lincoln. These salutes were never dry and formal; they were from the heart and made good reading. Nor did he ever forget to write a fresh and significant editorial on the meaning of the Seventeenth of May or Leif Erickson day.

An editorial in October spoke of the importance of the Norse Home project, one that would eventually become a reality as a retirement home for elderly Norwegian-Americans. "Do it," Gunnar wrote, "we need it." It opened in December 1937 with Abraham Kvalheim as president of the governing body supported by a board of prominent local Norwegian-Americans.

Chapter 10

THE HARD YEARS

Gunnar missed attending the gala opening of the Norse Home in December 1938. He had again suffered a stroke and was at home recuperating. The indications were for more troubles ahead but within a month he wrote to thank friends for greetings, flowers and many kind messages he had received during his illness. Though he hoped his condition was only temporary, he would never again be able to assume full-time editorship. He was happy that Ejde was in the office to take over the editorial responsibility, but he chafed at the conditions his doctor set for him: one pipe, one cigar per day, no more. His mind was fully active and he did considerable reviewing of exchange papers from the United States and Norway, and it was impossible to prevent him from taking short trips downtown to the office, usually with Marie accompanying him. This was especially true when he felt a major issue required an editorial. He wrote at home and then announced to Marie that he must make a trip to the office "no later than tomorrow morning." She would of course remonstrate, but at last give in.

Beginning that fall the indomitable Marie did her bit to provide copy for the paper. She started a series of thirteen articles on the goals and the activities that built the Daughters of Norway on the Pacific Coast.

In December the Valkyrien Lodge welcomed Betsy Kjelsberg as speaker at Norway Hall. She was billed as the "unofficial ambassador of Norway" and hailed as the highly successful president of the National Council of Women in Norway.

A young man of Norwegian parentage, Arthur B. Langlie, won the primaries in the Seattle mayoralty election. On the 11th of March, fairly bursting with pride, Seattle Norwegians celebrated the election of Arthur B. Langlie as Mayor. His next step would be election as governor of the State of Washington.

By early spring of 1939 the staff at *Washington Posten* was in an all-out frenzy of work preparing the largest edition in the history of the paper to celebrate its fiftieth year.

Bjørnson's beloved and most famous story, Synnove Sølbakken, made into a film in Norway, played continuously from 1:30 to 11:00 PM on Saturday the 5th and Sunday the 6th of March at the large Metropolitan theatre in Seattle.

Marie Lund's book *Dette er Norge* was voted first book to be read by members of the book club of Aberdeen's Lyngblomster Lodge, Daughters of Norway.

The 50th anniversary issue of *Washington Posten* came out on May 13, 1939 and in size it passed all expectations, a leap from the customary six or eight pages to a full 52 pages. As Ejde wrote in a jubilant editorial, "It is a tired but inordinately proud and grateful editorial department that sends out this celebratory edition. A hearty thank you goes out herewith to the many individuals and organizations that with articles, letters, telegrams and by many other means have made possible that this issue became what it is. And not least, thanks for the financial support in the form of advertisements!"

The first page, under a large picture of Stortingspresident C. J. Hambro, contained his message:

"On this 50 year jubilee I send to *Washington Posten* my sincere best wishes – and at the same time I wish to send a warm greeting to Editor Gunnar Lund with thanks for his capable work as a journalist and his faithful work in holding love for Norway alive among those who emigrated."

Gunnar's participation included one of his best Seventeenth of May editorials; a long signed one in large type spread across page one. It repeated in glowing prose the history of the day and why it is observed with such a rich outpouring of emotion. He pointed with pride to the fact that here in our own Seattle, in the furthest West, we have become the only immigrant group able to fill to overflowing the city's largest hall on our national day. And he concluded with a warm, "Congratulations on the heritage of the Seventeenth of May."

There were congratulatory messages to the paper from many West Coast organizations, from city and state officials, a signed one from President Roosevelt, and a full page of congratulations from the Norwegian Commercial Club and its members.

At the Civic Auditorium the fifty-year history of *Washington Posten* was featured as part of the annual Seventeenth of May celebration. While Gunnar was unable to attend for reasons of health, he was delighted to hear of it.

One discordant note in the 50th year edition was the announcement that in June *Washington Posten* would begin to publish a Scandinavian newspaper in English that would be combined with *Washington Posten* which would continue in Norwegian. This short-lived venture died within two months. From a news standpoint it was highly acceptable, but there had been no plan to build all-Scandinavian circulation or to cover costs through increased advertising. This was not Gunnar's doing. He was at home in failing health. His youngest son, Roald, as business manager of the paper, was responsible for the fiasco. Many years later another publisher would remold *Washington Posten* into a combined English and Norwegian-language paper and assure its survival.

Meanwhile, the resourceful Ejde assured his readers that *"Washington Posten will* continue." And it did.

The issue of June 17 reported that Leif Erikson Lodge No. 1, Sons of Norway, had honored its eleven living charter members by making them life members. The list: John Gaustad, Andrew Hansen, M. A. Hansen, L. H. Larsen, Oluf Larsen, Gunnar Lund, Edward Lystad, Gust Oseberg, Lars Relling, H. P. Rude and Olaf R. Sather.

In the July 22 issue it was reported that Yngvar Sonnichsen was dead. He was a 30-year resident of Seattle and the artist who had done the outstanding murals in Norway Hall.

C. J. Hambro, president of the Norwegian parliament and his country's delegate to the League of Nations, arrived in Seattle on a speaking tour. He lectured in Seattle, Vancouver BC, Everett, Tacoma, Olympia, Astoria, Portland, and Eugene and in California.

Inga Frodesen reported from Norway that Seattle's August Werner sang with the Chicago Male Chorus at the *Vi Kan* Exposition in Oslo and was greeted with a storm of applause.

Beginning with its August editions, O. L. Ejde finally listed himself in the masthead as Editor, a position he had filled for many months during Gunnar's illness.

On August 19 Nordlandslaget announced that the theatre it had purchased on Eighth Avenue and completely refurbished as a meeting hall would be called Harmony Hall. It was a major step for the organization of immigrants from the Nordland area of Norway. The Hall was dedicated in an open house that Ejde declared was conducted "in style."

With the October 7 issue the paper started a yearlong series in English from Norway by Dr. Sverre Arrestad of the Scandinavian department, University of Washington; his articles were a well-written, well-researched study of the economic and political situation. He would also spend almost a year in Denmark, Sweden and Finland writing a series about those countries as well before returning to the University in Seattle.

Ejde in a major October 14th article raised the question whether the local Leif Erikson festival should be "reconstructed or destructed." Some years before as a project of the Sons and Daughters of Norway it had drawn a respectable audience of 2,000 to the Masonic Temple. When the festival "went Scandinavian" it was at first highly successful, filling the Civic Auditorium with over 5,500 attendees, but the latest attendance was only 2,000, much smaller than any current Norwegian-only Seventeenth of May festival. It seems, he suggested, the Swedes and Danes have little interest in Norway's Leif Erikson.

On page one of the November 25 issue the paper told of the death of Queen Maude of Norway, mentioning her great popularity and the grief of the nation. On December 9 a front-page picture showed the palace flag at half-mast and great crowds of people gathered in front of the palace to indicate their sympathy to the King and his family and the sorrow of the population.

New breakdowns of the 1930 census gave Norwegian-born population by state:

Minnesota 268,000, Wisconsin 136,000, North Dakota 125,000, Illinois 81,000, Washington 77,000, New York 77,000, Iowa 57,000, South Dakota 56,000, California 49,000, Montana

29,000, Michigan 23,000, Oregon 21,000, New Jersey 16,000, Massachusetts 12,000. A total 1.1 Million (70.9%) were naturalized citizens of the U.S.

There were thus in 1930 147,000 Norwegian-born in the three states that comprised *Washington Posten's* prime circulation area, Washington, Oregon and California.

A half-serious, half tongue-in-cheek campaign to get *faar i kaal* (lamb in cabbage) featured regularly in Norwegian-owned Seattle restaurants was waged in Roald Lund's English language front-page column. The last report listed three takers: Hoseth's Snowdrift Café, Newgard's Reliable Coffee House, and Mrs. Schelland's Nordlys Café.

And in the January 20, 1939 issue, signed O.L.E. (O. L. Ejde), there was a light- hearted and delightful essay on the values of a wood-fired cookstove, headlined "Before Breakfast Philosophy." It started, "In my youth I had many faults... now I have only one." He confessed that every morning, first up in his home, he burns a mass of wood in the cookstove "for no reason but my own happiness and comfort." He continued for a full quarter-page giving the rationale behind this behavior, winding up with, "My kitchen stove, a wonderful and eternal institution. So grievous are things today that there are folks who have such a wood stove, but would throw it out if they could afford more modern equipment."

Ejde published one reader letter (of many) that lauded his deft touch, his whimsy, and his "elegant" style. The letter begged for more articles by O.L.E. As a result *Washington Posten* later printed a series of similar essays all signed "Pen Holderen" which we might define as a bad case of "mixa." But he wasn't fooling many of his readers. They recognized it as a pen name for Ejde.

On March 31 the headline "Ballard's Norwegian Navy

Prepares for Action as Halibut Season Opens" covered the rush to get the fleet under way as the season opened.

For weeks *Washington Posten* carried stories of the visit of Crown Prince Olav and Crown Princess Martha to Seattle and the Far West. As they neared Seattle there was full pomp and circumstance. At Fort Lewis a 21 gun salute boomed out, 8,000 American soldiers marched, and motorized units roared across the reviewing fields. The government of the United States of America was officially saluting Norway and the Crown Prince pair. The welcome Seattle Norwegian-Americans gave them at the Civic Auditorium was certainly quieter, but it was deeply felt. And their visit was a total triumph of simplicity and charm. A short paragraph in Roald's column about the Crown Prince pair summarized what many Norwegian-Americans thought about them:

"I remember Crown Prince Olav's face as he unveiled the pioneer monument at Stanwood. He put down the wreath, straightened up, read the inscription and bowed his head. Just as you and I would do on a dark night when nobody was watching us. That is one fortunate thing about being a Crown Prince. You can show your homage and emotions openly and people will love you for it. Olav and Martha of Norway, these home folks of ours who were with us so short a time, made us quite proud to be Norwegians."

In July the committee that had been organized to arrange the Civic Auditorium celebration for the Crown Prince pair cast up its final accounts. It found a surplus and made a decision that sparked grateful comment by both Ejde and Gunnar. The committee voted the surplus of $455.80 to *Washington Posten* in gratitude for its services. Ejde's reaction: "We have received the gift with inexpressible pleasure and consider ourselves fortunate to have Seattle as a hometown

— a place where mature, farsighted people of both sexes are at the helm."

In a separate editorial comment, Gunnar harked back to November 1905 when he took over the publishing of *Washington Posten*. He recalled that the successful effort to gather our Norwegian congregations and organizations into a united effort for our new country and Norwegian interests had been a major objective of *Washington Posten* in all the years since. He ended, "I would like to offer my heartfelt thanks to the committee for the gift and the appreciation it indicates for *Washington Posten's* efforts."

The gift, Ejde wrote, was an epoch-making event in the world of Norwegian-American newspapers. It was certainly most unusual, though there was little reason to expect that it would open up a new era of support for the struggling foreign- language press. Ejde pointed out that in 1939 there were not more than a dozen Norwegian papers surviving in the United States.

Since the first Norwegian-American newspaper was published, *Skandinavia* in New York City in 1847, an astounding total of 561 publications had been started. By the end of 1989, fifty years after the monetary gift, there would be only two Norwegian-American newspapers remaining: *Nordisk Tidende* (now *Norway Times*) in Brooklyn, NY and *Washington Posten* (name changed to *Western Viking* in 1959) in Seattle.

The list, compiled by Olaf Morgan Norlie in Northfield, MN (and published in the 100th year anniversary edition of *Western Viking* May 17, 1989) indicated that 41 publications had been started in Washington State alone, including Tacoma 14, Seattle 10, Ballard (now part of Seattle) 5, Spokane 6, Everett 4, Poulsbo and Parkland 1 each.

The story and editorials that *Washington Posten* published

concerning the monetary gift from the committee caused a flurry of surprised and enthusiastic comment in foreign language newspapers across the country. In Brooklyn, *Nordisk Tidende* congratulated *Washington Posten* and wrote, "In a time when it becomes increasingly difficult to publish a Norwegian-American newspaper, it is pleasant to see such an outpouring of understanding and good will." *Svenska Posten* in Seattle commented, "Seattle's Norwegian organizations are to be congratulated for their progressiveness." *Western Viking* in Tacoma declared, "Such a gift is completely unique in Norwegian history in America... We take off our hat to the men and women who made this gift possible."

During the last month of 1939 the nation watched with horror and sympathy as the USSR attacked Finland. It was of special importance to Roald who remembered walking the streets of Helsinki and admiring the modern architecture and the friendly Finns, but the major impact was his sudden feeling of revulsion. He had been under the typical liberal illusion that Stalinism and the USSR were the wave of the future. Now he knew communism was not the answer; it was the problem and a satanic one at that.

At a Civic Auditorium mass meeting in mid-December of 1939 Mayor Langlie, the Norwegian Male Chorus, Senator Schwellenbach and Dr. Friborg of the Swedish Baptist Church were on the program to raise money for Finland relief. Another all-Nordisk *folkefest* followed early in February 1940 with the proceeds to go to Finland relief. Seattle was not alone in this effort; the Norwegian Club of San Francisco raised $2,700 for Finland.

In January 1940 there was a call for the fourth annual conference of the American Committee for Protection of Foreign-Born. The cause was a rash of anti-alien bills in

Congress and growing discrimination and antagonism against the foreign-born reminiscent of the dark days of World War I. At that time the governor of Iowa by proclamation banned the speaking of any foreign language. Bills were introduced in many states including Washington. In Oregon such a bill was actually signed by the governor, which would have wiped out the foreign-language press. By March *U.S. News* was reporting that signs of another anti-alien crusade were accumulating rapidly and that nearly 100 bills directed at aliens were now pending in Congress.

There is strong indication of a cause-and-effect relationship between wartime hysteria and what we can call "reduced heritage action" as measured by the organization of new Sons of Norway lodges. During World War I there were no new lodges in the Pacific Norwest district and this continued for almost a quarter century until the 1930s. Then twelve new lodges were organized during the 30's before World War II when new lodge formation collapsed again. That condition continued through the Korean and Viet Nam periods. It was not until the mid-1960s continuing into the 90's that there was a real spurt in organization of eighteen new lodges. By that barometer, at least, there is evidence that "heritage action" rose and fell and was very sensitive to impact of anti-foreign-born activity.

Gunnar had often thought of the foreign-language press as a whole and of its role in the United States. He saw it as a transitional vehicle, enabling the enormous tide of immigrants to achieve an earlier and smoother understanding of America. He once said that the foreign language press was for the United States a fortunate accident. No act of Congress, no plan could have been more effective in encouraging the immigrant to become an American and in making him feel more at home here.

But he also finally recognized that the foreign languages the immigrants brought with them would fade out with succeeding generations. Though regrettable, this was inevitable. As the languages died, so would the foreign-language press. That also was regrettable and inevitable.

In the meantime, the fanatics had to be faced. In defending itself the foreign-language press was defending America and the successful process of assimilation and Americanization. He was proud of the role *Washington Posten* had played and pleased that he had been fortunate enough to be involved in what the paper had achieved.

Gunnar had many primary goals for his newspaper, though there is no record of his having written them. But through reviewing the 1,716 weeks over his 30 plus years of active editorship it is easy to see what he stood for. Here are the major issues, not necessarily in order of their importance in his eyes, except that the first goal did deserve its place at the head of the list.

We will publish a newspaper that vigorously advances the following causes:

1. Loyalty to the United States, its constitution and its aims in war and peace in deep gratitude for the opportunity it has given to the immigrants and their descendents.
2. Continued devotion to Norway, the land of our birth.
3. The unquestionable right of all Americans to preserve their heritage.
4. Recognition of the foreign-language press as the most positive influence for assimilation of the foreign-born.
5. Defense of the foreign-born against attack by ill-informed fanatics.
6. Greater Norwegian content in all our public programs and, especially, a united Seventeenth of May celebration in Seattle.

7. Building the Norse (retirement) Home in Seattle.
8. Building the Norwegian Hospital (This was the only aim that failed).
9. Full and continuing support of our Norwegian-American organizations.

It was an imposing list of aims and it required continued effort. It also required a continued balancing act. Could and should an immigrant maintain full loyalty to his adopted country and still cherish the memory and take pride in the achievements of the land from which he had emigrated? Gunnar did not find this inconsistent. One was a matter of political loyalty; the other was of the heart and memory.

Gunnar would have been puzzled by the multiculturists of the 1990s and beyond who were strong believers in teaching the children of immigrants in the immigrant language rather than in English. Gunnar had opposed such an idea back in the early 20's. He felt assimilation should be achieved as rapidly as possible. Loyalty was to be to America, but that did not mean that the immigrant must forget his native land and its culture.

Heartbreaking news dominated *Washington Posten* of April 12, 1940. Norway was under heavy German attack. One key incident marred the plan for the Nazis. In the dark early morning of invasion, April 9th, the German heavy cruiser *Blucher* came at full speed up Oslofjord to land the fifteen hundred troops that were to take over Oslo and paralyze the Norwegian government. But despite false orders to the Oscarsborg fort not to fire on German ships, it fired on the *Blucher*. The single shot tore the *Blucher* open and sank it with the loss of all but 40 lives.

That fortunate shot gave time to get the nation's supply of gold, the royal family and the government itself out of Oslo and eventually to England. However the respite did not enable Norway to repel the Germans, far from it. As the German noose tightened on the country, Norwegian-Americans pulled themselves out of their despair and did the most they could: a massive effort to guarantee whatever relief they could arrange.

On the morning of the invasion Roald came to his job as newscaster at KJR just before five in the morning. His was the task of preparing and broadcasting the first news of the day at 7:15. As usual, he first reviewed the night Teletype file from United Press, looking for major international news stories. Stunned by the invasion news, he continued his work, waiting until seven o'clock to be sure his mother was up. He dialed the familiar number Capitol 3082. Marie was cooking breakfast and answered the phone quickly, hoping that Gunnar would not be awakened. He was recovering gradually from still another stroke.

Roald's message was short, "Mother, something terrible has happened, Hitler is invading Norway."

She was silent a moment, then, "Oh no! Shall I try to keep the news from Gunnar?"

"You can't," Roald stated. "You had better tell him when he wakes up, rather than have him hear it on the news or see it in the headlines. I wanted you to know. I'm so sorry to bring you such bad news."

Quietly, she thanked him and hung up. She opened the front door and found the morning newspaper on the porch. She folded it to hide the first-page banner headlines and put it by Gunnar's place at the breakfast table. She whispered to herself, "How can I tell him? It will hurt him so dreadfully." She went upstairs to awaken him.

A few weeks later in *Washington Posten's* office in the Seaboard Building, Ejde opened the safe and took out the bound 1936 files of the paper. He flipped through the pages until he found what he was looking for, an article Roald had written while in Norway. Ejde reprinted it in full under a new headline "Who is Major Vidkun Quisling, the German's Norwegian Premier?" A follow-up on Roald's earlier scathing interview with Quisling, it told of the traitor's fantastic past history, how he had offered to build storm troops for the Communist and Social Democrat Parties so they could take over the government. The article had stated Quisling was a traitor, "probably a swindler, and certainly a high grade liar and no one ever accused him of having principles." Years later, when Hitler was defeated, the Norwegian government hanged Quisling. Few, if any, thought that too drastic a punishment for the man whose name, in virtually all languages, now means "traitor."

In the June 14th issue *Washington Posten* reported that the war for Norway was over. The Germans were in control. Over the years before the liberation of Norway the paper would report incidents of resistance heroism, the indomitable spirit of Norway's people, and the growing hunger as food supplies shrank. Here in the United States the immigrants and their descendents raised money for Norway relief, and waited. Crown Princess Martha and the children came to Washingon, D.C. where they were guests of President Roosevelt. The Crown Prince and King Haakon stayed in England with the Norwegian Government-in-Exile.

Storting President C. J. Hambro came to the U.S. on a speaking tour for Norway Relief in September 1940. In Seattle's Masonic Temple he drew an audience of 2,500 and many were turned away. The committee called him back and a week later he spoke a second time in the much larger Civic Auditorium with 3,000 attending. All proceeds went to Norway Relief.

On August 30, 1940 Gunnar celebrated his 75th birthday

with an open house in his home. Flowers, telegrams and letters streamed in together with many friends and deputations from a number of organizations. He looked surprisingly well and the event seemed to lift his spirits rather than tire him. An article in the Sons of Norway magazine commented on his birthday: "From the first, Lund has had a lively interest in the Sons of Norway and a significant amount of the Order's progress in the West is due to his contribution. As one of our organization's founders in the West and earlier president for the Second District and as the most prominent representative of the West Coast Norwegian-American press, Gunnar Lund must rank among our chief figures."

For just over two years, Gunnar had suffered a series of strokes that only permitted occasional trips to the office. On these infrequent trips Marie always accompanied him. At the end he was bedridden for several weeks. He died November 27, 1940.

Washington Posten reported that Gunnar was one of the oldest and best-known Norwegian-American journalists. With his purchase and leadership of *Washington Posten* the paper grew from a small number of subscribers to many thousands in cities and towns from northernmost Alaska to the Mexican border. Gunnar had led a very active life and among his activities were charter memberships in the Leif Erikson Lodge, Sons of Norway, the Norwegian Commercial Club of Seattle, and the Washington Newspaper Publishers Association. He was an honorary member of the Norwegian Male Chorus and Sigma Delta Chi the journalist fraternity at the University of Washington.

In the same issue that brought news of Gunnar's death, Ejde wrote and signed an editorial tribute. Mentioning his many years of working with him, Ejde declared there was one designation that best described Gunnar, "A gentleman and a scholar, a phrase that really does not belong to our time. Only in a metaphorical meaning can it even be used about a modern person. But it fits Gunnar Lund. There is something fine and old-fashioned about that expression, and there was much that was fine and old-fashioned about Gunnar Lund...

"Gunnar Lund was a proud man in the word's best meaning. He required respect and was respected by those who had any relationship with him. One reason was that he always obeyed his own rules, and one such rule included that everything must be done as well as he had ability to do it. He never left anything to the next day.

"With but a short interval I have worked with and for Gunnar Lund and *Washington Posten* since 1913. After all these years I can possibly best express my feeling by printing here the short telegram I sent him on his 75th birthday August 30: 'Congratulations on your 75th birthday and with the many useful years of which I also experienced such a rich portion'."

In the following issue there was a lengthy letter from one of Gunnar's old friends, Halvor Quam, who had worked closely with Gunnar in the old Arne Garborg club in Chicago and in the direction of the Sons of Norway District 2 Grand Lodge. At times he had the impression that Lund underestimated himself and his capabilities, and when in all friendliness he reproached him for this, Gunnar, with a whimsical smile, replied:

"On your level, on your level, not in the high blue sky,
There life has set your being, there shall you be tried."

(A very free translation of the Norwegian original quoted by Gunnar:

På det jevne, på det jevne, ikke i det himmel blå
Der har livet sat dig stevne, der skal du din prøve stå.)

That verse does much to describe Gunnar as he really

was: practical, pragmatic, realistic, fundamentally humble. He was not one to boast or brag. He had no false airs. He might have been the publisher and editor of a fine Norwegian-language newspaper who was knighted by the king of Norway for a life of service, but he never wore the decoration. It was tucked away in his bureau drawer. But he always wore his love for Norway openly, and he knew Norway would survive its wartime tragedy.

The things he treasured? His wife, his family, his home, his cabin on Puget Sound, his many friends, and certainly very high on the list: his work, the career he had struggled to find and to live up to its demands. It shaped and dominated his life. He never doubted that he was the luckiest man he knew. He was a man satisfied with the strict order and routines of his life and the hard work that it required of him.

He had his pleasures. There was Old Norse, his study of Icelandic. There was his pipe and an occasional cigar. There was in season the evening's peeled and quartered Winesap apple, his daily walk to and from work, the weekends in the crude cabin at Erland Point. There was his time spent with the Sons of Norway and his other organizations. There was his highly prized American citizenship and his participation in the democratic process. He was a man with great personal dignity. He had the immense good fortune to become wholly suited to his life's work and was therefore at peace with himself and his world.

Somehow, life went on for his widow. Marie had wrecked her own health in the two long years of caring for Gunnar. Yet, after his death, she went to the office almost daily to do what she could to take Gunnar's place. She was listed in the masthead as Publisher, but the paper could not have continued without Ejde's devoted work.

Finally, even the trips to the office became too much for

her. She died on September 16, 1943. Marie had the care of her old friends Carrie Aalbu and at the very end Martha Castberg, Ejde had the task of writing another Lund necrology. He reported that just a week before her death Marie had called to say she would surely be better in a few days.

"She was," Ejde wrote, "a leadership personality and her work in Seattle fell during the period when many young Norwegians came to the area. This was a time when her interests, capabilities and willingness to work found a rich opportunity for unfolding. Among the organizations that especially benefited by her efforts were Valkyrien lodge and the entire Daughters of Norway in the West, and to an even greater degree the Norwegian Hospital Association. She was president of Valkyrien and of the District Grand Lodge and she was president of the Hospital Association from its founding through all the years until her final illness.

"It was in her own home that Mrs. Lund was at her greatest. People usually knew her best as a speaker and leader or from her articles in *Washington Posten*. But a more competent homemaker is unthinkable. Her home was a sacred place where everything had to be perfect. She served her husband and children as if they were higher beings and the coziness and comfort she created were renowned. She was also a splendid hostess and through the years she made welcome in the hospitable Lund home many outstanding visitors from Norway.

"That her home and family always had first place characterized her as a woman. When several times she had to limit herself because of money pinch, it bothered her no more than a rain shower. It was something temporary which did not lessen her stately manner. When Gunnar became ill she dropped everything else to care for him. He needed all her hours, and therefore she naturally said farewell to all her dear outside activities."

On December 24, 1943, a front page box contained this announcement:

Salute to the New Publisher of Washington Posten

For the first time in 38 years the Lund name doss not appear on the masthead of Washington Posten, for with this issue ownership of the paper passes into the hands of O. L. Edje.

This is a difficult yet pleasant announcement for the children of Gunnar axnd Marie V. Lund to make. Washington Posten has been part of the Lund family since 1905 when Gunnar Lund purchased the struggling little paper that was, under his determined and spirited guidance to become the main voice of the Norwegian-Americans on the Pacific Coast. Through more than twenty-five years Mr. Ejde has shared the ups and downs, first as editorial assistant and, since the illness and death of Mr. Lund, as editor.

A foreign language newspaper is not a business venture, it is an obligation and a responsibility. Of this all three of us are aware, for we have all at various times worked in the office of Washington Posten and we are intimately acquainted with its mission and the devotion it has called forth from the men and women who have made it what it is.

Because our interest in its future continues, we are deeply gratified to announce that Mr. Ejde, as editor and sole owner, will carry on the work of Washington Posten. His efforts through the years were fully appreciated by both Mr. and Mrs. Lund, and it was their express wish that he be given the opportunity to acquire the paper. We are sure the subscribers and Norwegian organizations served by the paper will welcome this announcement in the knowledge that Mr. Edje will continue to publish a paper noted for its editorial excellence and service to its community.

Our sincere best wishes to O. L. Ejde and deep appreciation for his fine loyalty to Washington Posten and our parents. They would be happy to know that after their deaths Washington Posten continues in the old traditions and in the best possible hands.

John V. Lund
Helga Lund Algyer
Roald G. Lund

John Lund was acting head of the Journalism department at the University of California, Berkeley. Helga Lund Algyer was in Decorah, Iowa with her children, while her husband was in Colorado on duty with the Navy. Only Roald was in Seattle, on duty as a reserve officer at district headquarters of the Navy. He was the fortunate one who was able to take his father for walks until the end, and often be with his mother and he was the only member of the family able to attend the two funerals.

In his editorial column, Ejde welcomed the new era, writing that for him this was one of life's major mileposts. He stated that the paper would continue on the same course that Gunnar worked to follow. He recounted all the strengths the paper had and declared the best of these was the steady growth in circulation, plus the steady increase in number of Norwegian-Americans on the West Coast and the large circle of dedicated correspondents.

Ejde remained publisher for sixteen years until 1959 when, at the age of 70, he sold *Washington Posten* to Henning C. and Ragnhild M. Boe, although Ejde continued to write for the paper until 1967. Ejde died in 1971 at the age of 82, he had been associated with the paper for a total of 58 years.

Gunnar would have agreed that Ejde and Henning Boe were two of the finest owners possible for *Washington Posten*. Ejde provided years of top flight service and saw the paper through Gunnar's illness and death. Boe, an experienced printer but with no journalism background, took classes at the University and brought the paper a vision for the future – a new name *Western Viking* to give it a broader stance, an editorial policy that made English the predominant language, the reduction to tabloid size, a change to offset printing to cut costs and make pictures possible without cost, and a thrust to expansion by acquiring the subscription lists of failed Norwegian-American papers such as the venerable *Decorah Posten*.

As of the beginning of the 21st century, *Washington Posten* still lives as *Western Viking* with Kathleen Hjørdis Knudsen as editor and publisher. It is one of two remaining Norwegian-American newspapers. It survived through an era, dedicated to serving Norwegian immigrants and their succeeding generations.

Chapter 11

JOHN

In 1926 Gunnar was jubilant when his firstborn, John, decided he wanted a year of postgraduate study in Norway. John had taken some Norwegian at the University of Washington where he had majored in journalism. And since John was going to study Norwegian literature and history at the University in Oslo, it might mean that he wanted to perfect himself in the Norwegian language so that he would be ready to join his father. Did he want to know Norway's culture so he would be comfortable in eventually becoming the editor and publisher of *Washington Posten*?

Gunnar felt these were not the questions you asked your son outright. Better to cooperate and hope for the best. He asked the help of the Norsemen's Federation in Norway in getting John accepted at the University. John himself had applied and received an American Scandinavian Foundation Fellowship, but the major financial support came from Gunnar who told John he would send a monthly check to cover expenses. Marie gave John names and addresses of relatives in Oppdal, while Gunnar did the same for Stavanger. Both of them also supplied names of influential friends in Oslo. They felt it would be helpful if John explored his roots with relatives and developed relationships with top people in the capital city.

John had received academic training in a first-class journalism department at the University of Washington including time working on the University's daily newspaper. Then, following the advice of his journalism counselor, he had worked one summer for a neighborhood newspaper in Seattle and had stayed out of school for a full year to gain practical reporting skills as a staff member with the *Daily Olympian* at the state capital.

He had from childhood first-hand proof of the power and importance of the press. At age nine he had spent a rainy Saturday morning with his father at the *Washington Posten* office. On leaving they walked up to Second Avenue and were waiting for the No. 13 Summit streetcar when a large limousine pulled up in front of them. The back seat occupant waved to Gunnar and motioned him to get in. As John learned later, the affable friendly man in the back seat was U.S. Senator Poindexter. The Senator asked about Gunnar's health, how the big Seventeenth of May festival had gone and how *Washington Posten* was doing. He announced he was on the way to his hotel and as he was dropped off he ordered the chauffeur to take Mr. Lund and his son to their home.

As they pulled up before the Lund home, John noted that the neighbor boys and girls were playing softball. They stopped their game to watch the Lunds get out of the big limousine. John waved jauntily as he climbed the front steps to the house, delighted at the impression he and his father had made. During the next fall there had been a major meeting downtown to hear President Taft. John sat at the press table with his father, watching Gunnar and the other newspapermen taking notes on the speech. John then and there decided he would be a journalist. What other work had such prestige and importance?

For John, the year of 1936-37 was to be a time of graduate

study in Oslo. Gunnar had spoken to the agent for the Norway Pacific Line, who assured him they would be delighted to have John as a free passenger to Norway aboard the Norwegian freighter *Theodore Roosevelt* from San Francisco via the Panama Canal. Through an inexplicable misunderstanding, he was booked as a work-away, serving meals to the crew from 5 a.m. to 8 p.m. seven days a week. An added burden was that he had to buy his own blankets, mattress and towels. His demanding job continued for some weeks until the news came by radio from Norway that King Haakon had knighted a Gunnar Lund of Seattle, and that his family included a John Vognild Lund. John's duties changed immediately. He was elevated to assistant steward for the twelve passengers.

His trunk packed with summer and winter clothing for Norway did not reach the *Roosevelt*; it came two months later on another vessel.

His greatest disappointment was that the Oslo University was not then like the University of Washington or any other American university, where an almost unlimited range of courses were offered in American history and literature. In Norway it was expected one would get Norwegian literature and history at the *gymnasium* or community college level. The University had a different mission: educating professionals such as attorneys, doctors, engineers, government officials and would-be professors. After spending two semesters of self-guided reading in history and literature with only two courses of any real interest, John gave up in despair.

He did enjoy Oslo and Norway for other reasons, however. He took thrilling toboggan rides down the famous Corkscrew course with only minor injuries, he spent weeks at Brekstad near Trondheim visiting with his Aunt Anna

Wiggen and her family, and he saw great operas and plays in Oslo. He also saw the farms and the people of Oppdal.

At the urging of his farmer cousin Knut Dørum, he did his best to introduce young men in Oppdal to the American sport of basketball, drawing on his own experience playing for the Immanuel Lutheran Church team in Seattle. Years later he would often speak of the beautiful Oppdal farms, Dørum and Viken, and of his repeated visits there.

During his stay he wrote a number of excellent articles, all indicating his enthusiasm for Norway and the way of life he saw there. The articles appeared in *Washington Posten* in Norwegian, very probably translated from John's English originals by his father. During this period the paper rarely ran anything in English.

He was only fairly successful in polishing his ability to speak Norwegian well. He had not learned to write the language with any confidence. When he returned after his student year in Norway, Gunnar was anxious to know what to expect. Could he count on John joining the family firm?

While his father was in Norway along with eleven other American journalists John did spend five months working at *Washington Posten* as office manager, and during that period he was also asking questions and reviewing facts about the paper. Upon Gunnar's return John told his parents he wanted to talk with them about his future.

When he had planned graduate training in Norway, he believed he might on his return join his father and make the Norwegian-language newspaper his life work, but he had discovered too many problems with this future. Of greatest importance was that Norwegian was still a foreign language to him and he had only a surface acquaintance with some of the literature and little of the history of the country. He had not acquired any fluency in speaking Norwegian, let alone in writing it. In addition, the obvious fact of the sharp reduction in immigration greatly limited the future of the paper. Eventually there would be nothing left of the Norwegian-American presence but a second generation unable to read Norwegian. Current readers were almost all elderly. Circulation was shrinking. John could not see *Washington Posten* as the career he wanted. He carefully omitted saying that the Norwegian paper offered too small a future, too narrow a scope, and too little challenge. As businesslike as he had been in marshalling the facts and making his decision, he wanted to avoid hurting his parents, but in this he was not entirely successful.

When John was finished, Gunnar simply nodded his head. Later, alone with Marie, he confessed what she expected to hear. Gunnar was devastated. But within a few days he tried to be philosophical about John's decision. He reminded Marie that *Washington Posten* could only have limited appeal to John because there would always be the language barrier and the lack of real empathy for the immigrant experience. John was probably doing the right thing, Gunnar conceded. Marie turned away so Gunnar would not see her tears. She knew that Gunnar was trying to hide his own deep disappointment.

The next day John made an appointment with "Pa" Kennedy, the head of the Washington Newspaper Publishers Association at the University of Washington. John was specific in his request. He wanted to know if any good weekly newspaper in the state was looking for an editor, preferably a paper where an elderly owner might be seeking an eventual buyer. Kennedy mentioned three but suggested John concentrate on the Camas *Post-Record*, a very sound weekly a few miles up the Columbia river from Vancouver and Portland with an aging publisher who wanted a capable young man to come aboard and, if everything worked out, buy the paper on time.

John called Camas, made an appointment, and three days later came back to Seattle to report he would be moving to Camas to be the editor there, with opportunity to acquire the paper. Gunnar congratulated him.

Camas was then a growing mill town, home of a very large paper mill. Within a few years it was to become a boomtown, increasingly a bedroom town for people who worked in Vancouver or Portland.

Before the year was out, John married Josephine Jacobs, an effervescent and highly intelligent young woman. They had met in journalism classes at the University of Washington. John was on his way with the *Post-Record*, where the subscription and advertising revenue both increased markedly. Within five years John and Josephine owned the paper outright. The paper was prospering and the printing plant had more than doubled its volume and profits. To cap their feeling that it was indeed a great world, they had a bright young daughter, Laurel.

Not long after, John who had been working extremely long hours came down with a serious illness. He was in the hospital and was to undergo a pnuemothorax operation or collapse of one lung. Josephine telephoned the news to John's mother. Marie started dialing Gunnar's office phone number, then hung up the receiver. This was not something to tell Gunnar over the phone. She hurriedly changed clothes and took the streetcar to town. Her voice was breaking as she said, "Gunnar, John is in the hospital with..." She paused, then continued, "Gunnar, it's *tuberculosis.*"

It was a dread word they had never used since Marie's illness had driven the family to move to Alki Point so that she could undergo what was then called fresh air therapy.

Furthermore, they both believed Marie's parents had probably died of tuberculosis. Gunnar took her in his arms, "Marie," he sobbed, "It's the end of our world. What can we do?" he asked hopelessly.

"Nothing, Gunnar. Nothing. But he *will* live. I *know* that."

John survived, but it took skilled care and a long recovery including repeated trips to warm and sunny LaJolla, California, to rest and recover his strength.

Two problems arose over the succeeding years. First, John became a full-blown editorial supporter and personal activist for the Roosevelt New Deal in a community where the advertisers and purchasers of printing, as well as many of the readers, were staunchly conservative. Second, John began to long for a larger scope for his ambitions. He investigated opportunities with the University of California at Berkeley they needed a qualified instructor in advertising for the journalism department and John was negotiating for that job.

Josephine was opposed to John's activism in politics and feared he was damaging the future of the *Post-Record*. Furthermore, she did not want to move. The upshot was separation and then divorce, with Josephine getting the newspaper and John leaving for Berkeley. It was 1941.

John thoroughly enjoyed the academic life at the University, but he soon found that there was no suitable modern text on newspaper advertising. So, he wrote one. Prentice Hall finally published his book *Newspaper Advertising* in 1947. For many years it remained the definitive text in this field and was widely used in many university advertising courses.

When the United States entered the war, many of the journalism department people joined the military services. Because John was unable to pass the required physical, he was promoted from his position as an instructor to interim head of the department. In Berkeley he married Joan Taylor, a charming and gifted young woman.

By 1947 John had earned a full-year sabbatical, and he and Joan left for Norway to conduct an intensive study of the underground press which had played a dangerous and resourceful role in supporting resistance to the Nazi occupation. Within a few months they had conducted dozens and dozens of interviews and had amassed a full file of wartime underground papers and notes. They had just begun turning their research into a book when they received a surprisingly large royalty check on John's newspaper advertising book. Its sales were far beyond John's expectations. The mail also contained flattering reviews of the book. One that seemed especially important at the time was an enthusiastic review from *Editor & Publisher*, the leading trade publication of the newspaper industry. With such reviews and high volume book sales, John saw a positive impact on his professional goal, a career as a university professor of journalism.

By January 1948 the fascinating underground press project was put on hold for a more pressing opportunity. John and Joan had become fascinated by Norway's approach to its social and economic problems. They saw many of the bold political and economic experiments in Norway as of high interest in view of present world trends and the heightening face-off between capitalism and communism. Could Norway's novel program be a compromise solution elsewhere? Could it have meaning for the United States?

They knew their book on the underground press could be done later when they returned to the U.S. It was of timeless interest and could wait but what they both saw was a current window of opportunity for a book to be called *Norway and the Third Alternative*. Time was of the essence. That book had to be written now, they had to have the final manuscript in hand when they arrived in New York in mid-August.

A letter home on February 3, 1948:

"We are up to our ears in books, reports, statistics and interviews with oceans more to come. We are now working on the first rough draft, we have written the publisher's man in New York and told him of our change in plans. Now we have to produce. Please, no discussion of this to anyone. "

They met the all but impossible schedule. By mid-May they had submitted copies of the polished manuscript to a panel of Oslo experts, including the Assistant Secretary of State, for evaluation and suggestions. They sailed from England on August first but advance copies of the manuscript had been sent earlier to their contact in New York. Upon their arrival they called him. He was enthusiastic about the book but said that his publisher did not go for it. He suggested Harper's, where they found interest and left a manuscript. Then they canvassed other leading publishers, leaving a few more copies of the manuscript behind them. There was nothing more to do except wait.

Norway and the Third Alternative was never published. Looking back to 1948 we may be guess the reasons. The impressive research data seems flawless, and the manuscript was more than a good first-cut, presenting a mass of data on the innovative steps Norway had taken in an effort to solve its unique political and economic problems. Many of those problems resulted from the years of occupation during World War II. The manuscript fully and accurately described the course the Labor Party administration was taking, which was a centralized planning and welfare state approach but this should have presented no real barrier to publisher interest.

Perhaps of greatest importance in their failure to find a publisher was that a similar story had been told in *Sweden*

The Middle Way, an extremely successful book by Marquis W. Childs. It was published by Yale University Press in 1936 and republished in a revised edition in 1938, with still another new and enlarged edition in 1947. The publisher was startled to discover that one edition after another sold out almost before it was off the press. The last revised edition was published just one year before John and Joan had tried to market their manuscript in New York. It was likely that no publisher felt their book had sufficient potential to compete with Childs' highly successful book. It is also possible the publishers felt the public was losing interest in a "Scandinavian third solution" to the capitalism vs. communism question

On the way home John and Joan stopped in Washington where John made calls on the State Department, expressing his interest in joining the U.S. Information Service. In Scandinavia he had seen what the USIS was doing and became intensely interested in its role in the new cold war, but he had not forgotten that he still had a position back at the University of California in Berkeley. He knew that his notes on the Norwegian resistance press could help him get a doctorate and ultimately a full professorship.

Months later, assuming the USIS was not interested in him, he accepted an offer of associate professorship from the University of Iowa. He and Joan moved to Iowa City and were in their second year there when John heard from the USIS. They had a first billet for him in Finland.

John had always wanted a job that would entail important work where he could fight in major battles. This was the opportunity to promote the United States and its democracy and the lure of playing on a big, demandingly difficult and highly important field.

Joan and John worked as a team. She learned the foreign

John and Joan Lund meet Dalai Lama II — New Delhi, India 1960.

languages and entertained the important people; John did the patient, endless task of trying to coax foreign nationals to understand and appreciate the U.S. in a world where the Soviet Union was the enemy and the battle was to outmaneuver and outplay the communists. He had found a career that could frequently be frustrating, but in the main was enormously fulfilling and utilized every shred of his initiative and determination.

After his years in Finland learning the complex job, he had a long string of important posts: years in Iran during the last period of the Shah, six years in India, six months as a traveling inspector for the USIS, several years in Washington, D.C. as head of the European Division of the *Voice of America* broadcasting to the Soviet-occupied nations of Europe, and finally several years in The Sudan.

John and Joan spent many of their vacations in Norway

Gentleman farmer in Spain: John Lund at the finca, *Santa Eulalia Del Rio — Ibiza, Spain 1966.*

and also came home to Seattle and Berkeley to visit family. They also visited nearby alluring places, such as a month on a houseboat in Kashmir. One of their unforgettable vacation sites was the Spanish Balearic Island of Ibiza. When John resigned after the African posting, they bought an imposing country home or *finca* on Ibiza for their retirement.

John became a gentleman farmer, growing fruit and vegetables that he sold to fancy restaurants catering to the tourist trade. In a trip to the United States, he stopped in Portland to see his younger brother and named as one of his objectives the purchasing of some exotic vegetable seeds and berry plants. Roald took him to a major seed packer's retail store where John selected sweet corn, Blue Lake beans, pole peas, burpless cucumbers and many other common American seeds as well as Marion blackberry plants.

"You call these *exotic*?" Roald asked.

"They will be in Ibiza." John replied. And of course they were and gave John an even greater edge with his demanding customers.

It was during these years that Joan started writing a book built around the strong religious experience she had in India. The book was completed in manuscript form but despite the efforts of John and his brother, a publisher could not be found. She was an active member of the Ibiza Episcopalian congregation and spent much time in ecumenical work, trying to bring harmony and cooperation between the Catholic and Episcopalian faiths.

As John recalled, "She became almost diaphanous. There was increasingly something unworldly about her; she seemed to be existing elsewhere, in some other realm. When she died, the local Roman Catholic priest asked for the privilege of holding the funeral in his church. The Episcopalian minister agreed. It was an unheard of event and a marvelous tribute to her."

John returned to the United States for a lengthy visit. Two years later he married Sheila Horlick, a vital English woman who had retired to Ibiza. In 1965, with advancing age and concern about health care on the Spanish island, they prepared to move to the United States. Prior to their move, Sheila saw that John was tending a large fire outside and went to find out what he was burning. He confessed it was his notes on the Norwegian resistance press.

"John," she exclaimed, "How could you do such a thing, after all your work?"

" I never got around to writing it, and now it's too late. I'm too old, too tired," he explained.

After a tour of the United States to find the perfect retirement location, they settled in Chapel Hill, North Carolina. John preferred it because it was a college town, there were many retirees drawn by the pleasant climate, and it was close to what John still saw as the center of his universe, the State Department and the USIS.

In Chapel Hill John founded a current events discussion group of about twenty retired men, all of whom had held executive jobs. They spoke of John as a gifted discussion leader who had a broad and accurate understanding of our country's problems. They were greatly impressed with his ability to organize discussions, his fairness, and his determination to overcome any and all roadblocks.

John's parents expected great things of him, and he did not disappoint them. To his sister and brother who had grown up with him he was an enigma. They envied his obvious talents and his dedication. They admired him, but in their early years they had not been as close to him as they were to each other. It was not until they were grown and had scored some achievements of their own that they could bridge the gap they had constructed.

They always held him in an awe that was to increase during the years. They told each other he was above their level in competence, in hard work, in single-minded attention to being successful in all he did. But they also saw him as lacking a sense of humor, and as a detailed thinker who had no time for nonsense.

At the end, they felt he had lived a highly productive, almost triumphant life. They wished they had tried harder to know him. They admired the friendships he had made and the respect he had won from so many of his acquaintances. He died just weeks before his 90th birthday. His wife Sheila held a champagne "celebration of life" for him.

Helga's husband was ill so she could not attend but Roald attended and told her of the event, "I shouldn't have been surprised. The house was absolutely jammed with people, some from his discussion group but packs of other people. They all seem so impressed with what John had accomplished and what he stood for. He was quite a person," Roald said, "How did it take us so long to realize it?"

As a boy, John did have his willful streaks. Once Gunnar, aggravated to his limit, told Marie, "That boy is stubborn."

"No, Gunnar," she argued, "You mustn't say such a thing. John is not stubborn, he is just determined and that is a very good characteristic."

He was acting out that "determination" at the dinner table one evening when his father happened to refer to his children as young and promising Norwegian-Americans. John objected strenuously, "I am *not* a Norwegian-American, I am an *American*."

Gunnar was angered. He snapped, "I don't want to hear that kind of disrespectful talk from you. You will apologize!"

John looked at his father stonily and said, "I won't. I know what I am!"

"And I know what you are going to get, a good whipping!" Gunnar arose from his chair and started toward John.

John jumped up and circled the table with Gunnar following him. Suddenly evading his father's grasp, John ran from the dining room and up the stairway with Gunnar following him. John escaped into the bathroom and locked the door.

Gunnar began pounding on the door, shouting, "If you don't open this door immediately, I'm going to break it down and come in and thrash you!"

Marie came panting up the stairs to hold Gunnar's arm. "Gunnar, don't break the door down. John is the only one in the family who can fix it."

Marie was correct. When Gunnar had to open a box of apples, he used a screwdriver and a hatchet, and the result was usually dire. He had little aptitude with tools or anything mechanical.

By the next day the storm had blown over and John apologized. But the other children, Helga and Roald, had both observed the fracas. For them the "Norwegian-American problem" was not over. It would disturb them both until they, like John, worked out their own solutions.

Chapter 12

HELGA

A quick look at the many events in Helga's life might give the impression that she was immensely lucky. A longer look adds this certainty: she was ready to perform, for she made the show go on, time after time. At 93 years of age, serene and fulfilled, she looks back with gratitude. Her life was indeed a richly good show and she had enjoyed it all. As she said, "Other than people, the loves of my life have been acting and writing." She had made a name for herself in both activities.

She was christened Helga Cecelia Lund; her middle name was the name of Gunnar's sister. Helga was a history-rich Nordic name.

Her mother, who also had a flair for dramatics, saw natural talent in Helga. From the Erland Point days, Helga had developed and performed skits. With her friend Sylvia Stub she had played dozens of these impromptu shows for an appreciative audience of children. She seemed to be a born actress. Her second talent was equally strong; she was also a fluent writer. To give Helga formal training, her mother arranged for her to attend Columbia College of Expression in Chicago.

There, the president of the College congratulated her, "Helga Lund! What a splendid name for a professional!" The name "Helga" had been an embarrassment when she was younger, it was foreign, unfamiliar, strange to many people. Helga had suffered with it until that day in Chicago. Suddenly her name became a treasure, something that would look very good in lights, something that would sound strong and memorable.

At the end of her first college year she took the train to Minneapolis to meet her father who was attending a very special Norwegian-American celebration, the centennial of the landing in New York of the little sloop *Restauration* from Stavanger. This small ship brought the first group of Norwegian immigrants, the beginning of a flood of almost a million immigrants who would become Americans. President Calvin Coolidge was the main speaker at this Minneapolis event. Helga sat in the press box with her father. It was for both of them a memorable affair, but for her far the most significant event of the trip happened on the train home.

Helga became concerned over two restless young girls whose mother was trying unsuccessfully to quiet them. Story telling was one of the skills Helga had learned at Columbia College, so she offered to tell the girls a story.

They were enraptured with "The Little Grey Mouse and The Little Brown Sausage," but suddenly Helga became aware she had lost eye contact — the girls were looking over her head. Helga paused with her story, turned, and saw behind her a handsome young man, who smiled and asked, "You must be Helga Lund, aren't you?"

"Yes, but how did you know?" she replied.

Still smiling, and looking at the little girls, he pleaded, "Please finish the story, we want to find out how it ends, don't we, girls?" They nodded and he sat down next to them.

He was Durwin David Algyer from Decorah, Iowa. He was on his way to Leavenworth, Washington, to work for the summer in the bank there. Earlier he had been in the observation car where he happened to talk with Helga's father, who told him about his daughter. In September Durwin came to Seattle and took Helga dancing at the Olympic Hotel. This chance meeting on a train lead to a major event in Helga's life.

Dressed in her Norwegian national costume, Helga rode on one of the floats in Seattle's big celebration of Norwegian immigration centennial at the University of Washington stadium. When she was much younger she had worn the costume to be the bride's sister in a portrayal of the Bridal Voyage in Hardanger. She also had worn the costume at innumerable Seventeenth of May celebrations of Norway's Constitution Day.

Helga saw Durwin again in Chicago during her second year at Columbia College and again in New York when she was returning with her mother from their long and memorable tour of Norway. The year was 1930 — a very special year in which Norway commemorated the death of St. Olav in the battle of Stiklestad nine hundred years before. St. Olav was the Viking king responsible for the Christianization of Norway.

Marie was writing for *Washington Posten* a series of articles that were later to be published in a book titled *Dette er Norge* (This is Norway). It was Helga's task to type the Norwegian language articles on her portable typewriter from Marie's handwritten copy. This was no easy assignment for Helga, whose command of Norwegian was minimal at the start of the trip, but in the two months of working together her Norwegian was greatly improved.

Marie and Helga made an effective team. They were very much alike. Helga had her mother's sense of the dramatic, the same ability to reach quick empathy with others, and the same uncanny ability to see and describe an event. For

Helga these aptitudes would be of great benefit in the work that was to open up for her in the future.

Their travels in Norway had taken them from Oslo to the northernmost part of the country, with stops several times at Brekstad to see Marie's sister Anna Wiggen and in Oppdal to visit the farm to which Marie had come from Russia as a young girl. During the trip Helga wrote a series of weekly articles for the *Seattle Post-Intelligencer* and one of them inspired the headline "Seattle Girl Meets King" which covered the interview Helga had with King Håkon of Norway.

On the way west, Marie and Helga stopped in Decorah to visit with Durwin's parents, just in time to participate in a concert program organized for the benefit of the local hospital. Marie spoke about Norway and Helga performed the Åse's death scene from *Peer Gynt*, supported by Carlos Sperati and the Luther College orchestra with music from Grieg's Peer Gynt Suite. Decorah had earned its position as the cultural center for Norwegian-Americans: the famous *Vesterheim* museum is there, as is Luther College, an institution endowed by the Norwegian Lutheran Church. Decorah was also the home of *Decorah Posten*, in its time the Norwegian-language newspaper with the largest circulation in America.

Back in Seattle, Helga created a series of original dramatic presentations she called *Monodrama*s that she presented on a tour arranged by a booking organization. She performed in the Seattle area and as far afield as Victoria and Vancouver, British Columbia. These engagements were not only successful, but they served to polish her stage presence and deepen her sense of the dramatic. As a result of these appearances, she was hired by the Bon Marche department store to write and broadcast a daily morning radio program as well arrange and be master of ceremonies at noon luncheons and style shows. She also acted in a radio station's evening serial, playing the part of a Norwegian maid with an authentic Norwegian accent.

One evening Helga and Marie attended *Juno and the Paycock* presented by the newly formed Seattle Repertory Theater Company. Helga was fascinated by their work and curious, wondering if there might be a chance that she could join them.

The next day she went to the office of the group. As a result she played the part of Sister Amy in *Little Women,* their next production. Subsequently she performed lead roles in a great number of plays including Ibsen's *Wild Duck, The Master Builder,* and *Peer Gynt,* as well as Chekhov's *The Cherry Orchard* and Pirandello's *Six Characters in Search of an Author.* For five years Helga played lead roles with the Repertory Theatre Company. After building its own theatre in the University District of Seattle it became known as the Seattle Repertory Playhouse. In addition to her acting, Helga also taught basic drama to the apprentice acting group at the Playhouse.

Flattering reviews of her stage work appeared in both Seattle newspapers, but those in *Washington Posten* were Spartan in their simplicity. Gunnar Lund might report that Helga Lund played a starring role, but his native reticence would forbid him from publicly lauding his own daughter. Yet he was delighted with her acceptance and popularity and would affirm this within the family circle. He was especially impressed when Helga was chosen to instruct drama classes at the University of Washington.

In 1937 a chain of circumstances intervened to put an end to Helga's stage career. A mutual friend Helen Field told Helga she had heard that Durwin still kept a picture of her in his room. Helen urged Helga and Durwin to come to her Detroit area home for a Thanksgiving reunion. The invitation was welcomed by both of them, and they were married shortly after at the stately Reeve home in Lawrenceville, New Jersey. Their first home was on prestigious Beekman Place in New York. Durwin was with the investment-banking firm of Eastman Dillon. Later he became a partner in the firm of Goldman Sachs and Company.

Another set of happy coincidences opened up a new career for Helga. She received a letter from a college friend, suggesting she call radio actress Alice Frost who was to star in the popular soap opera *Big Sister*. Before Helga could make the call, Alice Frost called and invited her to have lunch during which she asked about Helga's stage and broadcasting background.

Alice relayed the information about Helga to Stuart Ludlum, head of the McCann-Erickson radio department. He soon called Helga and invited her to come to his office for an interview.

"I've heard so many good things about you that I don't need to see your scrap book," he said.

She laughed, "That's lucky for me. Unfortunately, my scrapbooks were lost forever following a train trip from Minneapolis to Seattle . I drove around town all night with a detective but never recovered my luggage. So you'll have to take me at face value."

"That's good enough for me," he smiled. "Would you rather act or write?"

She thought a moment, and aware of the demands acting in a daily show might make on her marriage, responded, "I'd rather write." Ludlum briefed her on the new radio soap opera, *The Romance of Evelyn Winters*, to be sponsored by Standard Oil of New Jersey. The site of the series would be precisely where Helga was living, Beekman Place. Ludlum asked her to write a trial opening script. She did, he liked it, and she was hired.

Later she also wrote the series *Career of Alice Blair*. For a script in which the leading man was to go blind temporarily, Helga donned a blindfold for several days, "just so I could write about blindness with a deepened sense of how it felt."

Early in this period she told Mr. Ludlum she would like to attend rehearsals but he advised her that the actors and actresses were usually opposed to such an idea. Pressing the point, she arranged a luncheon with Alice Frost who had been active in getting Helga involved in the writing assignment.

"Alice," Helga said, "You know I've done some acting back in Seattle. As a general rule, I had a copy of the play at least a month before the opening show. I had two tasks: one, learn my lines, two, understand the play and my part so I could interpret it according to the author's original vision. Radio is different. I write the script, which you see, only an hour or two before airtime. It's your job to make the part live. I'd like to help.

"If I watched some rehearsals, could I do a better job of writing to the styles of the actors? That would make it easier for you because the lines might better fit you."

Alice was enthusiastic, "That's an angle I never thought of. Makes sense! Let's give it a fair trial. I'll brief the other cast members. Join us for next Monday's rehearsal. Is it a deal?"

Helga said, "Thanks, but first let me check it out with Stuart Ludlum." Through her writing she met many Broadway actors and actresses who were also appearing on radio soaps. Casts on her own shows included Toni Darnay, Karl Weber, Ralph Bell and Alice Frost in *Romance of Evelyn Winters*; Joseph Cotten, Martha Scott, and Shirley Booth in *Career of Alice Blair* and Josephine Hull in *Meet Miss Julia*.

She wrote these radio serials for about three years with a total of several hundred episodes, plus a number of evening shows. All this work was as a free lancer with McCann-Erickson, Air Features, Young & Rubicam and Frank and Anne Hummert.

Helga and Durwin had two daughters, Deanne and Marilyn. The family's stay in New York ended abruptly when America went to war in 1941. Durwin became a Lieutenant in the Navy, assigned to the supply department at the ammunition depot in Hawthorne, Nevada. Helga and the children moved to Iowa where they lived in Durwin's childhood home. Before she left New York her script assistant Phyllis Cerf (the name she took after she married Bennett Cerf of Random House) suggested to King Features that they engage Helga to write the novelized version of the *Blondie and Dagwood* comic strip. She wrote the book while "durationing" in Decorah. When the war over, the family returned to New York until Durwin took early retirement and they returned to Decorah where he managed their large farms. He also served as investment and financial advisor to Luther College. Helga was very active as a board member and vice president of Vesterheim Norwegian-American Museum in Decorah.

Durwin died of a heart attack and, with both their daughters married, Helga moved to Sarasota on the gulf coast of Florida. There she starred in the lead roll of *I Remember Mama* with The Players and brought to it an easy and authentic Norwegian-American dialect. Reviews were deeply satisfying.

Sometime later Helga moved to Naples, Florida where she received a telephone call from Durwin's long time friend in New York, James Stuart Parsons. He had just heard of Durwin's death and he asked permission to fly down to see her. When he arrived he simply announced that he planned to "take care of her." They were married shortly after and took a six-month

*Helga — Greensboro,
North Carolina 1997.*

trip around the world. They spent their summers at his second home in upstate New York. During the winters they lived in Naples for a number of years and then moved to High Point, North Carolina. Jim was an inveterate world traveler and took her on a series of cruises, one of which carried them to Norway. At Trondheim Helga arranged for her cousin (the daughter of Marie's sister) and her family to come aboard the cruise ship for a luncheon. In Oslo she was captivated by their stay at Holmenkollen Hotel, high above the city in the same area as the world-famous ski jump.

After Jim's death at the age of 90 Helga moved from Naples to Greensboro, North Carolina, to be close to her daughter Marilyn.

One person Helga never lost contact with was her

younger brother Roald, who had moved from Seattle to Tigard, Oregon. They spoke by phone almost every week. She came west in the early fall of 1995 with her daughter Marilyn to participate in a Norwegian-flavored Lund family reunion there. Helga's daughter Deanne came from San Anselmo, California, and grandchildren and great grandchildren came from Roseburg and Eugene, Oregon, The celebrated guests from Norway were Tore Viken who now operated the Viken farm and his school- teacher brother Erik. The two of them were members of the many times national champion Norddafjells Oppdal Spellmanslag, a folk music group. Both had brought their instruments for a reunion concert. Effortlessly Helga played her own role, the Grand Dame of the Lund family. She munched Norwegian delicacies, talked with everyone, and added that dramatic, queenly presence that was so natural with her.

And in one-on-one conversations with Roald after the affair, the main topic was family memories: Marie, Gunnar, Erland Point, *Washington Posten*, the early days in Seattle and the close family bonds they both so appreciated.

"When are we going to start doing something about writing the family story?" she asked.

"One of these days, maybe," he replied, "Maybe."

"Remember brother, if we don't, no one will. And that would be tragic." She smiled. "Think about that."

Chapter 13

ROALD

On December 14th in 1911 Roald Amundsen discovered the South Pole. Early in 1912 the news came to the world and was reported in *Washington Posten*. It was a time of rejoicing for Norwegians everywhere and especially for Gunnar Lund. He had known Amundsen during his student years in Christiania. Roald Amundsen, Gunnar noted, had proved to the world a Norwegian could be first. So when Marie gave birth to her third child on May 12, Gunnar felt it entirely fitting that the boy should be given the name Roald.

Roald is not a name an average American can pronounce with ease or correctly. As an example, Miss McCabe in her Broadway High School freshman class in ancient history announced with some pleasure that she had a boy with a famous name, "Will row-ALD please stand? I'm sure he was named after the famous explorer row-ALD aMUNDsen." The "a" in ALD was pronounced like the "a" in absent — which Roald would rather have been.

He can still remember a first-grade recess at Lowell Grade School. A group of boys circled around his next door neighbor Steig Gabrielsen chanting "Stig Stig sat on a twig" while Steig cried. These were the penalties of being a Norwegian-American. While hardly life threatening, they could make life miserable for the shy and sensitive. That

187

may explain why Steig changed his name to Steve, why his brother Earl had his last name legally changed to Gibson, and why Roald invented and used the nickname Ru and used just R. G. Lund on business cards and letters throughout his business career.

Gunnar had the habit of calling Roald "boy" as in "boy, keep faith with your feet" when Roald deliberately walked out of step with his father. There was one time when Roald remembered the "boy" with pleasure. During the summer of 1930 when Marie and Helga were in Norway, Roald spent much time alone at the Erland Point cabin.

After lunch one Friday he decided to saw up a large old growth log back in the woods on the family property and if he possibly could, finish the job before his father arrived in the late afternoon. The outer part of the log was punky and made the saw pull hard, but he kept on sawing although he was covered with sweat. When he finished the final cut and wiped his forehead, he was surprised to hear his father's voice ask with amazement and considerable pride, "Is that *my* boy?" Walking quietly, Gunnar had arrived early from the bus stop and had been standing there for some minutes, watching.

It was an accolade Roald never forgot and from it he learned a value that Gunnar held firmly — work was a higher good, especially when the work was hard and when you kept working despite the need to stop and rest.

There were other values. One was that you did not crumple a newspaper, you treated it with respect. Books must be handled with loving care for the printed word, in any form, was to be honored. One did not leave food on one's plate, there was something holy about food and it deserved much more than plain respect. Like the printed word, food was sacred.

In the summer of 1930 Roald and his friend David

Anderson paddled a canoe from Erland Point out past Bremerton and south on Colvos Passage, down the Tacoma Narrows. They portaged across to Hood Canal, paddled around Foul Weather Bluff and returned to Erland one week later. During the previous summer Roald had backpacked alone into the Olympic Mountains and over Quinalt pass before returning to Erland, foot-weary but exhilarated by the glory of the mountains. He was becoming a confirmed loner.

Living with an editor of that period automatically inclined one to turn toward a communication field. John became a journalist. Helga became an actress and a writer. Beginning in the fifth grade Roald published a one page household newspaper typewritten by the hunt-and-peck method.

It was natural that Roald should take journalism at Broadway High, winding up as an editor and columnist on the school weekly that won the coveted All-American award. Now he felt sure he would be a journalist.

In 1936 after the sale of the Erland Point cabin Roald went to Norway for almost a full year and wrote a weekly two-column article in English for his father's paper. He was 24. There were many adventures to report, none more treasured than time spent working on the age-old farms of his relatives in Oppdal. He saw northern Norway aboard the *Coastal Express* and went ashore at Vardø where his mother had been born. In Oslo he enjoyed friendships with such celebrities as the brilliant young poet and patriot Nordahl Grieg who was to die while on a bombing run over Germany.

In Oppdal his closest friend was the young farm hand Harald Nyhaug who later married the Viken daughter Marit and took over the farm. It was in Oppdal that Roald met and fell in love with Marit's friend Aslaug, a tall lovely girl whose blonde hair had a touch of red. Leaving Oppdal he

Roald in his Navy days — Seattle, Washington 1945.

continued travelling to Sweden, Finland, and the Soviet Union. In Moscow he received a cable from his brother John telling him his father had suffered a serious stroke and asking him to come home immediately. There was two-way correspondence with Aslaug, but that waned with time.

After his return to Seattle Roald met Edna Humphrey who was in her senior year at the university. She was bright, delightful company and mutually attracted. They were married the following summer. Roald's work at *Washington Posten* and his participation in Norwegian-American organizations and social life increasingly disturbed Edna. To her his ethnic involvement was uncomfortable, strange, and even threatening. Meanwhile, he was still deeply depressed over his folly in attempting to convert *Washington*

Posten into an English-language Scandinavian publication. When he was offered a position as news editor and newscaster at a radio station he accepted, feeling it would save his marriage and also make his work-life happier. After two years he left the radio station to become editor of the *Herald*, a weekly in the small Washington coastal city of Raymond. This position, lasting only a year, was terminated by his call to active duty as an officer in the Naval Reserve after the attack on Pearl Harbor. He was stationed in Seattle at Thirteenth Naval District offices.

Erik Humphrey Lund had been born in January 1941. John Carlyle Lund was born in October 1944.

Roald was transferred to New York, and when the war ended he had negotiated a contract to write a newspaper soap opera for radio. It lasted just 13 weeks, and then Roald went back to radio station work as a program director in Seattle.

These were years of heavy reading. His father had set the stage, convincing him of the significance of the written word. That influence was heightened by Roald's friendship with Harry Hartman, widely know as Seattle's blind and best bookseller. Harry's shop was across Fifth Avenue from the building where Roald was a newscaster. Their friendship blossomed and the bookseller became a strong influence as to what Roald read. Harry introduced him to the books of the philosopher George Santayana, which started Roald on a lifetime of reading in philosophy. Later in his life he became interested in economics, political science, current events, and what he celebrated as the American defeat of Soviet communism.

A week after Roald's return to Seattle from New York and the navy, Harry called asking him to come downtown for lunch. Roald was trying to complete a radio script that had to be in the mail that evening. He protested but Harry insisted it had to be that day. Roald agreed, hoping he could finish the script by early evening and then make a second trip to town to catch the last mail for New York. At the bookshop, Harry took Roald's arm and they walked to their favorite deli. They talked about New York and Scribners, the publishing house where Harry's written introduction had made it possible for Roald to get out-of-print Santayanas. Harry had no special message nor was there any urgent reason for the lunch meeting that day except that he simply wanted to get together. That night Harry suffered a fatal heart attack.

Roald began a series of jobs that later reminded him of his father's fifteen year hunt to find his life's work. Reaching the same goal took Roald twenty-five years, including the five years he spent in the Navy. He did not have to do manual labor as Gunnar had done in his searching years. Roald worked in public relations for an insurance company, sold advertising specialties, and worked for two separate advertising agencies. He became a partner in a radio and TV advertising representative business that on a flip of a coin carried him and his family to Portland to open a branch office for the firm. The coin- flip decided which partner must move to Portland; Roald lost. He next worked in sales management and marketing for a brewery for three and a half years. This was the longest he had spent in any of the fourteen jobs he had held since he was 18. After graduation from high school he had moved from job to job out of frustration or boredom. He was 50 years old before he realized the importance of making a change, a permanent change. He knew he must find his life's work.

With unabashed presumption, he decided to become a consultant, assuming he could help business leaders solve their problems. Even in those days consulting required at least a college education with an MBA preferred. Roald had no degree and no knowledge of how a consulting company operated, but three years later he was head of a three-partner management consulting firm, a board member of the national Association of Management Consultants, and about to become a founding member of the accrediting Institute of Management Consultants.

Initially he found and worked for the business type he knew best, radio station owners. His thrust was marketing, which included training sessions with the sales manager and his salesmen. He started in smaller markets such as Pendleton, Salem, Eugene, Medford, Chehalis-Centralia, then into larger markets such as Seattle, Tacoma and Portland. After he added a specialty in market research he soon gained recognition as a marketing consultant. This growing capability put him into marketing for stainless steel, titanium and manufactured metal products such as pumps and valves. Food manufacturers followed. By the time he had three years experience he added management consulting to his services and eventually that became his dominant type of work.

Edna and Roald had graduated to their second home in Portland, a grand, older home in Eastmoreland where there was space for Edna's parents to visit them. Her father, Warren Humphrey, and her mother Camille, were model-perfect grandparents, and they drove frequently to Portland from Seattle especially to see their grandchildren.

On the day when Erik reached sixteen, the legal age for a driving license, he offered to drive his mother on an errand. She had backed the car out of the garage and he had closed the garage door. Edna moved over and Erik climbed into the driver's seat. Then, unfortunately, he shifted gears into "low" and gunned the motor, a mistake that caused a six-hour repair job to the garage door. From then on when Erik was again allowed to drive he was always reminded: "R is for Reverse."

On another occasion Edna had completed baking her hermit cookies, a family recipe that had been acquired by her grandmother from another woman when their wagon trains had met on the way west at Keosauqua, Iowa. Edna left for a trip to the grocery store, leaving the dozens of cookies on the kitchen counter to cool. John tended to be slightly chubby in those days and was not to eat snacks. While Edna was away he came home from school and went out to play. When Edna came home there were two cookies left on the counter with the note, "I was hungry – John." Edna had a moment of panic, then found the cookies, all of them, neatly placed in cookie jars.

John had an early love affair with radio possibly growing from the wooden microphone his father had made for him. At the age of 14 he had a carrier current station (Radio KAOS – the teen-aged voice of Eastmoreland) on which he broadcast to homes within a two-block radius. By age 16 he and his buddy were holding down the weekend shift at a radio station in Kelso, Washington. Not many years later John and his wife June established a highly successful firm of consultants to radio stations with offices in the San Francisco Bay Area.

Erik became a management consultant, joining his father for some years and then opened his own consulting firm and teaching marketing courses part time at Portland State University. Earlier, Erik had married Helga's daughter, Deanne Algyer. They had three children, David, and twin girls Kärin and Kristin. The marriage ended in divorce and later Erik married Carol McEwen and the couple had a daughter Britta and a son Erik who became a professional basketball player in Norway then later in Denmark.

One of Roald's specialties in his consulting practice was holding one-company team seminars for individual firms on the subjects of management planning, strategic planning or marketing planning. He developed this unique seminar concept out of dismay over the standard "open" seminars where a mixed audience from various companies was normal. In such seminars generalized knowledge was the best one could expect. To make his seminars more practical he aimed them at a team from a single company, first familiarizing himself with client problems. At the seminar itself he took three days to pound in the technology and apply it to the client company from the thick customized notebook. The team then went back to company jobs for two weeks or more with heavy "homework" assignments. When they returned for the final two-day session the homework was turned into a written plan specifically for that company. These became popular, practical for the clients and quite profitable seminars.

At one point he did depart from his "one company team" principle to conduct three-day "open" seminars in Boston, Chicago, and Los Angeles on marketing of consulting services, sponsored by the Association of Management Consultants.

Ten years after his startup as a consultant he left the company he founded to return to the preferred life of a solo consultant. He and Edna had earlier acquired three acres on Bull Mountain 12 miles south of Portland near the city of Tigard. There they built a home with a sweeping view out over the coastal foothills. He modified his tractor barn into a unique office and thereby cut his commuting time to less than one minute to cover the distance of fifty feet from home.

Those were heady years. He performed a major research assignment for the Russian Amtorg Trading Company to discover why Midwest American farmers were no longer buying Russian-made Belarus tractors. The answer was simple: many of the first wave of these stout but outmoded

Roald as Management Consultant — Portland, Oregon 1995.

tractors were rusting in American fields (and also in Soviet fields) for lack of replacement parts. In its wisdom the planned economy of the Soviet Union manufactured tractors in one plant while another company in another city made parts for the tractors. The parts plant was inefficient and unable to keep up with the deluge of orders.

His other clients included a major bank chain, high technology companies, food products and heavy equipment manufacturers. One of his long-term clients became the world's largest dental equipment company. Many of his clients were located in the east or California which necessitated his traveling a minimum of two weeks or more a month.

CHAPTER 13 – ROALD

Despite his heavy travel schedule, he and Edna gardened joyously and finished a five-year landscaping job in one year without hiring any help. It was a life they both loved. On a summer evening, working after dinner until dusk, tired and sweaty, they retired to easy chairs on the western patio to enjoy the view out over the Tualatin Valley to the Coast Range and the glorious sunsets.

One day he called Edna from his office, asking her to pack his bag for a redeye night plane to Boston. He also asked her to cancel his date for an annual physical and arrange for a later appointment.

Edna did not cancel the date but kept it for herself. When Roald returned home from Boston a week later, she confronted him with serious news. "You'd better know this," she said, "I took your physical. I have lung cancer."

They smoked their last cigarettes on the way to the hospital. He knew Edna should not come home following her surgery to find him still smoking. So he packed away his pipes and on the following day he cancelled all clients requiring travel. Edna endured a rough operation and weeks of radiation, but the cancer had metastasized. There were hard months of chemotherapy that left her weak and her bones brittle. She fell breaking her pelvic bone. In the hospital, she died of a heart attack during the night.

He continued his consulting work, learning to his chagrin that he could equal his out-of-state consulting billing by staying home and concentrating on the Portland area alone. Later, he married Carol Waters, a Californian whom he had met at a seminar. In 1987, half a century after his year in Norway, he booked a vacation trip to Norway for the two of them which included a voyage on the *Coastal Express* to northern Norway, visiting relatives in Oppdal, Trondheim and Oslo, and seeing again his father's hometown of

Stavanger. It was a great plan, but the tickets were cancelled when the doctor reported Carol must have a major operation for cancer. Three years later he was alone again.

After five decades of neglecting Norwegian, Roald started reading the language again. His first book was *Sophies Verden* the novel by Jostein Gaarder that became a world success and was published in English translation as *Sophie's World*. He held a dictionary in one hand, the book in the other, and read aloud to teach himself the language he had almost forgotten. When he exercised, he counted aloud in Norwegian to re-learn numbers. In April 1995 he left for the trip he had planned with Carol. It was 58 years since his 1936-37 trip. He was 83.

The language facility returned gradually, even many words in the strong and wondrous Oppdal dialect. While visiting in Oppdal, he learned that Aslaug, the girl he had loved, had died, speaking of him with her friend Marit before the end. He could only close his eyes and shake his head.

Harald, the farm hand who was his close friend in Oppdal, had died in his forties. He and Marit had two sons, Tore who now ran the farm and Erik who taught school. They were big, handsome men. Roald enjoyed them and their Norwegian folk music. They were members of the renowned folk music group in Oppdal.

In Trondheim he met the engineer son of the farmer with whom he had taken a memorable winter sleigh trip to the summer farm *(seter)*, over half a century before, He met again his two cousins Aslaug and Maisa, daughters of Marie's sister Anna. They were now in their upper eighties. He met their two grown children, one an educator, the other a psychiatrist. In Stavanger he met a distant cousin who showed him the graves of his grandparents and his father's childhood home.

It was an unforgettable eight-week trip. He carried with

him his laptop computer and portable printer. He wrote nine articles about his travels for *Western Viking* - the successor to his father's Norwegian-language weekly – now printed largely in the English language.

How, he asked himself, had he allowed himself to forget Norway during the past 58 years? How had he permitted building a business and a home to all but eliminate this important element in his life?

In early August he called his cousin Tore in Oppdal. "Tore," he said, "If I were to send you tickets, would you and your brother Erik like to come to Portland for a visit?"

Tore responded quickly, "You must be joking!"

He bought the tickets through his Norwegian travel agent, Berit Johanson. In preparing for his Norwegian visitors, he asked Berit if she knew of a Norwegian caterer in Portland since he was planning a homecoming dinner for his family. Berit told him there was none. Then she added, "But my friend Åse Barnes and I will prepare the dinner for you just for the fun of it." Wearing their Norwegian folk costumes, they prepared and served everything from pickled herring to the festive Norwegian crown cake.

The two cousins from Norway were the centerpiece for the reunion. They were taken on a full day's trip to the coast, discovering loggers' quantity and quality of American pancakes at Camp 18 Restaurant then inspecting and admiring the huge American logging equipment at the open-air museum. They enjoyed double scoop ice cream cones at Tillamook Dairy and superb pizza with poured honey for the crusts at Neskowin's Hawk Creek Cafe. A long walk on the sandy beach down to Proposal Rock preceded their drive back to Bull Mountain through the Van Duzer Corridor of huge Douglas fir trees. The next days they visited wineries and drove up the Columbia river to the famous old Columbia

Gorge Hotel for the seven-course ranch breakfast where they heard of Simon Benson, the well-known Norwegian immigrant who had made good in the logging business and had built the hotel. They were fascinated by their visit to a Columbia River salmon hatchery, one of many operating in a vain attempt to save the badly depleted salmon runs.

On the final Sunday Tore played his accordion and Erik his fiddle for a Norwegian folk music concert at the Lund homecoming party with Helga, children, grandchildren and great grandchildren attending. Tore and Erik presented Roald with the classic Norwegian sweater their mother Marit had knitted for him, a sweater he wore to every Norwegian event he attended for years to come, delighted with the pewter clasps, softness of the yarn and colorful collar.

Touched by the gift, Roald wore the sweater most of that homecoming day, warm as it was. When evening came, rather than hang it up, he folded it almost reverently and put it into the old red-painted Oppdal chest his mother Marie had brought from Norway over a century before. They were, he knew, well mated.

For him, Norway had totally resurfaced in his life. He filled the family room of his home with Norwegian prints and artifacts. One of the great pleasures of his life was financing trips for two of his married grandchildren and their spouses for two-week trips to Norway. They came home ecstatic over Norway. He felt he had finally repaid his parents for his own first trip to Norway and had wiped out some of his personal losses through his long period of forgetting the land of his heritage.

Two years later he was planning another trip to Norway through his travel agent when Berit noticed a coincidence, "You are making much the same trip as another client of mine. You are both going to Fjærland on Sognefjord, a place very few people from here visit."

When Berit called to tell him his tickets were ready she set a date with lunch to follow. He arrived at the travel agency to find Berit working with an attractive woman who was the other client going to Fjærland. Berit introduced him to Ilamae Vinje Warnes who was also of Norwegian parentage. The bond of common heritage developed and a short time later they were married. Ilamae made her scheduled trip to Norway with her son, daughter and granddaughter. Roald arrived later and spent time in Stavanger before meeting Ilamae at Vik on Sognefjord after her guests had left for their homes in the United States.

Together they experienced the round-trip voyage on the Coastal Express ship Nord Norge and visits to Vinje in the Voss area, Trondheim, Oppdal and the south of Norway.

Returning to Portland, Ilamae and Roald moved into his home which now had its own "Norwegian room" — the family room he filled with Norwegian art. Within a few years it was also to have an authentic *kubbestol*, a traditional carved chair made out of a log.

His wife had gone to Fjærland because her son wanted to see the famous glacier there; Roald went to Fjærland because it was Norway's first book city, with thirteen used bookstores in the village. He sent home packages of his plunder, the complete Norwegian-language works of five major Norwegian authors.

When Roald had formally retired from his consulting business in the late fall of 1995 he held a retirement luncheon with nearly a hundred former clients attending, but he continued to serve one client two more years. He was fully and finally retiring at the age of 85 after 37 years of consulting. The life work he had finally found had ended.

Looking back, he could recognize that his early life had

been strange, plagued by his own lack of decision, purpose or resolve. He had missed the higher education he wanted. He had drifted from job to job, never fired, but always dissatisfied. There had been early promise, but he had squandered it. For twenty-five years whim rather than purpose and resolve had ruled him.

After formally retiring he did not wonder how he would spend his leisure time. There was a large garden that needed tending. There were books to read — many of them including those in English that far outnumbered his Norwegian books.

In 1999 the need that struck his father before him now struck Roald with similar urgency. The same need that caused so many city-dwelling Norwegians to find themselves a *hytte,* a cabin on the fjord or in the hills, motivated Roald and Ilamae to buy a cabin on a cliff above the ocean with an unobstructed view of the Pacific. Roald saw it as a potential second Erland Point. It was to be their refuge from suburban life where they could fall asleep with the roar of the Pacific surf. There they could spend unrushed hours watching their resident bald eagle, Ernie (so named because eagle in Norwegian is *Ørn*) fishing with plummeting dives just inside the churning surf. It was a place where they could watch winter storms rush in and the whales romp on their way north to Alaska.

Somewhere, half lost in his memory, he could recall a fragment of a Norwegian poem he had read in his youth. "...For the sea, for the sea, my spirit is yearning, where it tosses and foams in endless churning..."

For no real need or reason, Roald splurged on a new laptop Macintosh computer. At the beach that fall he spent his first hours on his new laptop outlining a book that he suddenly remembered needed writing and had been postponed for many years. When he returned home he called his sister at her retirement home in Greensboro, North Carolina.

"Helga," he said, "I'm sending you a chapter-by-chapter synopsis of the book we never got around to writing. I call it *Our Enduring Heritage*. Let me know if you think I ought to go ahead with it."

Chapter 14

THE HERITAGE

We three children of Gunnar and Marie Lund — John, Helga and Roald — had a natural and self-imposed formality in our relations with our parents. We never used such familiar expressions as Mom or Pop. Even when we were very young we never used Mama or Daddy. They were always Mother or Father when we spoke of them to each other. We never used their first names when speaking of them, they were not Gunnar or Marie to us, they were Mother or Father. When one of our parents spoke directly to us or called us in from play, the automatic answer was always "yes, Mother" or "yes, Father." We did not need a stylebook to tell us that Mother and Father should be capitalized. It came naturally for us to do it. That is the way we always thought of them, and still do.

In some ways you might think Gunnar and Marie came from New England, for, like *Washington Posten* during the Depression, ours was always a "make do, wear out, do without" family. In the 20's and 30's the Seattle daily papers had what they called Society pages, a section of the paper that spoke of the doings of prominent women in the community. We overheard many times Marie's standard reply to a society editor of the *Times* or *Post-Intelligencer* who called to ask what she was wearing to a given concert or other event.

Her response was always the same. She laughed, "My

twenty-year old beaded black dress." And it was the truth.

Not that Marie was "society," but her chairmanship of a chapter of the Music & Art Foundation, plus all her many Norwegian activities and her zealous Liberty Loan work during the first World War apparently achieved a high visibility and respect that earned her the rank of "prominent." This qualified her for a presence in the society columns of the day.

When Father sent Roald down to Anderson the Norwegian shoemaker to have his shoes stitched together, the shoemaker scowled and said, "Again? You tell Gunnar this is the last time!" *Washington Posten* was not a money machine. John later suggested that Father was not the world's best businessman and he was probably correct. Making money or becoming rich was not Father's goal. He had other motivations.

If need arose for something important, such as education for the children or sending one of them to Norway, Mother suggested we "scrimp" for that purpose. In looking back, it is obvious that Mother was the one who did the scrimping. Not on food, but in not buying anything for herself or our home. Note that our family never owned a car. "Why should we put money into such a luxury?" Father asked, "We live only two blocks from the streetcar line." He never mentioned the more pressing reason: he was apprehensive of anything mechanical. He laughed at the thought of his learning to drive, and so did we.

We never thought of our parents as "pinchpenny" with us, their children. We enjoyed such frills as Boy Scout uniforms and celebrating Christmas with a tree under which there was always no end of presents. We ate well and we had the summer cabin at Erland Point but there was no ostentation in our home or our clothing. We probably couldn't afford it, but we doubt that we would have lived a "showy" life even if there had been extra dollars around. It was simply not the custom in our family.

John recalled what Father had told him: "We won't be able to leave you children money, but you will have your heritage."

"Our heritage?" Helga and Roald asked John what he thought Father meant by that.

"Probably our trips to Norway," John replied. He was prone to be crisp, matter of fact, literal-minded and authoritative.

"There must have been much more than that," Helga objected. She was the most discerning member of the three offspring and reaching beyond the obvious was her normal way.

"I wonder what he was thinking of," Roald offered. He knew his father occasionally spoke in visionary terms with obscure or multiple meanings.

John smiled with tolerant amusement. "Well, Father did indicate it was up to us to figure out what he meant by 'heritage', and that we'd understand when we were older," he finally admitted. Then he continued, "Father told me once that we come from a family that have been doers on both sides, that we come from a rich background, a country high in art, literature and music, and that the Norwegians are freedom-loving people. But he never really explained what he meant by *our* heritage."

By the time we were ready to deal seriously with this question, John was gone. Only two of us remained to solve the riddle Gunnar had left us. As a start, we explored the meaning of the word "heritage" itself. What did the great Norwegian-American authors Rølvaag and Ager say about it? Both of them tried to define it, unsuccessfully we believe.

O. E. Rølvaag, the preeminent Norwegian-American

author, wrote a book about our heritage as Norwegian-Americans, published in English translation by the Norwegian-American Historical Association under the title *Concerning Our Heritage*. A salient quotation:

"As citizens, we are Americans and only Americans. But in ancestry, in descent, in kinship we are Norwegians and can never be anything else no matter how desperately some of us try. I for my part can only believe that it is an eternal truth that our people came here originally from Norway. Therefore we are Norwegian in descent ... As I understand it there are riches and possibilities here which we have scarcely tapped."

In that book he seemed to concentrate only on the language and the behavioral and physical characteristics and customs he saw as Norwegian. He apparently found it impossible to enumerate these "riches and possibilities" in the actual ways enjoyed by many of the descendants of the immigrants

Rølvaag ignored genealogical research and getting in touch by letter or telephone with relatives in Norway. He did not think of travel to Norway to meet relatives and see the land of our forebears. He made no mention of Norwegian artifacts such as inherited chests and other items of Norwegian folk art. He did not mention enjoying Norwegian visual art, or folk costumes, or folk dancing, or even Norwegian food. He could hardly have guessed how many Norwegian-Americans participated in *rosemaling* (Norwegian folk "tole" painting usually with a rose motif) or Norwegian woodcarving and other active folk arts.

He also failed to anticipate that many, many descendants would find a home in such organizations as the Sons of Norway and the Norwegian Male Choruses or participate in broader Scandinavian heritage organizations and attend immensely popular Norwegian and Scandinavian festivals held in almost all parts of the country.

Rølvaag would probably have been both amazed and delighted to learn that a number of descendants of Norwegian immigrants became paying members of the Norwegian-American Historical Association, getting and reading the Association's excellent studies of the immigrant experience.

Waldemar Ager, the publisher of the newspaper *Reform* and author of many novels, was quite wrong when he wrote, "Experience has proved that with the decline of the Norwegian language, interest also falls for the rest of the ancestral heritage... If the language falls into disuse, then the interest for things Norwegian also dies... "

Ager is quoted in *Cultural Pluralism versus Assimilation* edited by Odd Lovoll. In a sweeping warning Ager wrote: "I myself have to confess that I have yet to meet a single person of Norwegian descent who cared anything about the ancestral heritage and ancestral culture unless that person also understood the Norwegian language."

Happily and perhaps surprisingly, the facts seem to indicate that as the language died among the descendants of the immigrants there was almost an inverse result. Though few of the descendants were proficient in the Norwegian language, "interest for things Norwegian" grew. What the concerned prophets failed to anticipate was the powerful, enduring attraction of the Norwegian heritage. It may not be manifested exactly in the forms Rølvaag and Ager hoped for, but it is very much alive, as it surely deserves to be.

To cite some impressive statistics: in 1895, the heart of the immigration period for Norwegians, the Sons of Norway was founded in Minneapolis with 18 charter members. In 1920 the first English-speaking lodge was formed in Chicago, a trend that was to become the norm for all the lodges. In 1945, over 20 years after immigration had been cut to a trickle, there were 24,000 members. By 1970 the order had not gone into decline, it had *more than doubled* to 55,000 members, 260 lodges and $75 million in life insurance in force. The order celebrated its 100th anniversary in 1995 with 400 lodges, nearly 75,000 members and an astounding jump to $750 million in life insurance in force. And the order went into the twenty-first century with an increase to 421 lodges,

This almost incredible *continuing* growth in number of members and lodges was certainly aided by lodge formation in smaller cities where there had probably never before been any trace of a Norwegian-American organization.

Is it so surprising that as the immigrants die the Sons of Norway grows? The second and third and subsequent generations have not forgotten "their heritage." It is, indeed, an *enduring* heritage. The descendants of the immigrants are actively seeking and finding their heritage in any of the multitude of ways there are to relive and enjoy it. At the same time, it is highly questionable if a substantial percentage of these current members actually speak Norwegian. The president of a major Pacific Coast lodge suggests 10 percent would be the top estimate for his lodge.

But the major question remained for us: exactly what could Gunnar have meant when he spoke to us children of *our* heritage?

We decided the best course was to look at our parents' lives and their values and search for clues there. Naturally, we saw first the obvious source of their devotion — Norway itself, their "homeland."

We had all traveled there. John had lived, studied and worked there twice for a total of two years. He had also been there on at least half a dozen shorter visits while he was stationed in other countries. Helga had spent a spring and summer there with Marie in 1930 and had a total of five visits to Norway. Roald had spent a year there in 1926-27 and returned for lengthy visits in 1995 and 1997. All of us children had been there on the family trip in 1914. What we three remembered as our peak experience was meeting the relatives, visiting the old farms we had heard so much about from our parents, and experiencing Norway.

Norway is a magnificent adventure, which explains why so many tourists from all over the world vacation there; but if it is the country of your own people, it has a special appeal far greater than the scenery. This, you say to yourself, is where my parents were born; this is where my grandparents lived and worked. This is the stunning beauty that surrounded them. This is what so many emigrants were compelled to leave because there was no future for them in Norway. This land of their birth is the reason why, in the United States and Canada, they formed and attended Sons of Norway lodges, and *bygdelags* (organizations by emigrants from specific Norwegian districts). This is why they gathered for *lefse* and *lutefisk* feasts, organized Norwegian Lutheran churches, and made pilgrimages home to Norway. No wonder they returned to Norway as often as they could afford.

Small wonder, too, that they kept things from back home — pictures of people and places they could never forget, a bit of jewelry, a miniature Norwegian flag on a brass pole, a tool from a remembered farm or a kitchen implement used in making *lefse* or *krumkaker*. Norway is a country where the venerable farm culture has produced weavings, woodcarving, the intricate folk art of *rosemaling*, regional costumes and rich folklore. We have no illusions that Norway is better than any other country of family origin, but in our case, it is the remembered and revered place.

To Decorah, Iowa, people of Norwegian descent come from all parts of the United States and Canada to visit *Vesterheim Norwegian-American Museum,* a treasure house of immigrant history. There they see dozens and dozens of immigrant chests brought from Norway in the nineteenth century and compare them with the one they remember. They also see an impressive wealth of other reminders of immigrant days. They visit the Nordic Heritage Museum in Seattle especially to see the brilliant and emotion-charged permanent exhibit of the immigrant experience, *The Dream of America.*

Why? Because they want to get in touch with the lives of the immigrants, lives that have enormous meaning for them and cannot be allowed to slip away.

For so many of us descendants of these immigrants our heritage includes remembering our people, the country, the language, the flags waving on the Seventeenth of May when Norway celebrates its Constitution Day. The remembrance is most vivid for the immigrant group itself, paler with the second and third generation even if they have made the pilgrimage. Paler yet with those who have had only one Norwegian parent or grandparent. The heritage, then, can be relative to the immediacy of experience. Heritage is a matter of connecting to all or any of the many things that define "Norway" for us.

These obvious elements of heritage were not difficult for Helga and Roald to identify and agree upon. But the elements of heritage that are far less apparent, the elements that deal with the characteristics and traditions of the people are more obscure.

Here we found it difficult to differentiate between the characteristics of the Norwegian people as a whole and our parents in particular. Certainly some of the characteristics we saw in our parents were widely shared. We saw strong evidence that they represent national characteristics.

Helga quickly pointed out that both our parents were

extremely hard working. Once they had taken on a task or mission, they applied sustained effort to complete the task. She mentioned Gunnar turning over the earth in the orchard at Erland Point; heavy shovel after shovel, with hardly a pause or sawing stove wood by the hour with no rest breaks. We could not remember him exerting a flurry of effort and then backing down when he saw he could not easily achieve a goal. This trait also applied to Marie, who would take on a gigantic task such as organizing elaborate events like the Wedding Party in Hardanger, grandly staged Seventeenth of May programs, or the Immigration Centennial Pageant, or the daunting challenge of building a Norwegian Hospital in Seattle.

Many of the people who came here from Norway were courageous and hard working. They knew from back home that nothing could be achieved without determination to survive, endure and keep going. As a result, many of them prospered.

This sustained effort of our parents we also saw mirrored in our own lives. John displayed it time and time again. He was a methodical workhorse. Helga poured out radio scripts day after day with great creativity and the ability to meet tight deadlines. Even Roald developed this characteristic as he grew up. Facing tough, lengthy processes in a consulting assignment he patiently ground out the hours of work that had to be done and made certain the result was quality work. Any one of us might be unhappy with our first effort and do the work again, driven by an inner necessity. Helga once told her nephew John, Roald's son, "It's a family trait, to work with such intensity that the rest of the world thinks it is insanity."

All three of us learned that our big satisfactions came from doing the difficult and doing it well. We had no question as to where we learned to think of work this way. Often we had the eerie feeling that one of our parents was watching and nodding approval or that if we didn't work hard and long enough they might be watching with disapproval.

We knew that Gunnar was an agnostic and yet we saw him as a very pious person. He had his own deep and abiding awareness that food, work, and nature were all sacred, a kind of earth piety we admired and adopted as our own. Marie, on the other hand, was a devout believer. Just before she died she asked for the sacrament of communion from Pastor Stub. He came, to her deep gratitude. Mother was a Christian, and she lived her faith quietly and effectively. Her acts of charity and caring for those in need never surprised us. We grew to expect that of her.

We three children went our separate ways, but none of us forgot the simple table prayer we learned from our parents and prayed in Norwegian:

I Jesu navn går vi til bords
Å spis og drikke på ditt ord
Deg Gud til ære, oss til gavn
Så får vi mat I Jesu navn

A simple English translation:
In Jesus' name we go to the table
To eat and drink by Thy word
Thee God to honor, for our gain
We receive this food in Jesus' name

This prayer is still a part of our normal ritual at family gatherings. However, it is probably correct to say that for most of us it is less a religious statement than a way to touch what we call our Norwegian heritage.

Gunnar started another family tradition, the formal dinner speech to honor any event of family significance. He stood up after such a dinner, fondled his watch chain, rapped his glass with a spoon for attention, and then commenced his brief and somewhat oratorical discourse. One such occasion was John's going to Norway for his year of graduate study at the University in Oslo. Another was Helga's leaving for college in Chicago.

One event of great family significance came at the dinner Marie gave in our home for Roald Amundsen and crewmembers of the *Maud* after completion of their historic voyage through the Arctic ice. This was a momentous occasion for Gunnar. He spoke of bravery, of Norwegian tradition, and of the great pleasure it was, in this far outpost, to welcome these stalwart examples of Norwegian manliness. They applauded him heartily. We children were impressed but hardly surprised. Father had scored, as we expected him to.

This speechmaking tradition has not been abandoned. All of us children have continued it. We may have lacked some of Father's classic style, but we dutifully followed his example of making an event special and memorable through homespun formal oratory.

Another tradition that has been followed enthusiastically is the serving of Norwegian food. In Father's day there was always a five-pound block of sweet brown *geitost* (Norwegian goat cheese) on the breakfast table. He applied it thoughtfully to a slice or two of bread. The cheese was thinly sliced with a Norwegian cheese plane (a slotted knife that is carefully drawn across the top of the cheese). For the children, the quantity might be reduced to a quarter-pound loaf of cheese in their homes, but again the special cheese plane. This treat is now enjoyed primarily at coffee breaks on thin *Kavli, Ideal* or *Mors* unleavened flatbread. There must be many who enjoy this minor feast, for both the imported cheese and flatbread are sold in a great many supermarkets here in America and probably in all stores in such centers of Norwegian-American population as Minneapolis and Seattle.

Pickled herring is another cherished traditional food, also best with flatbread. *Lefse* (the thin, moist potato bread) covered with butter, sugar and possibly cinnamon, is a Christmas holiday favorite. Christmas time also calls for the traditional Norwegian holiday cookies — *fattigmann, berlinerkranser, spritbakels, mandelstenger* and *krumkaker*. It would be almost sinful to forget *julekake,* the rich Christmas bread loaded with glazed fruit. Nor can we ever omit *tyttebær,* the Norwegian name for wild cranberries. Food is the universal tradition that speaks of national ancestry and helps keep the memories alive.

There were other traditions the three children preserved: typical phrases such as *takk for maten* (thanks for the food) the simple but heartfelt gratitude that is expressed after every meal; *vær så god* (be so good) the invitation to the dinner table or to a passed dish of food, and, on greeting a Norwegian friend, *takk for sist,* (thanks for the last time).

Mother particularly loved to make things festive, or *å være koselig* (to be cozy) to enjoy the moment together. Looking back, those moments were indeed festive and they are remembered. They typify the Norwegian flavor she gave us in our lives together.

Gunnar left another tradition with his family. We may have seen him as a "professional Norwegian" because most of his work was reporting what was happening in every part of Norway every week as well as among the Norwegian-Americans in virtually all their communities on the West Coast. But he was really a "professional American" also, participating in his adopted country's democracy as well as taking a patriotic editorial stand. He rarely missed the opportunity to write a heartfelt editorial on the Fourth of

July and on the birthdays of Lincoln and Washington. His was no split personality, we saw him as profoundly American, glad he was here, devoted to this country's democratic principles, bringing to it the best characteristics of his people. For his children following his ardent Americanism was easy and natural.

In our search we covered many examples of what "our heritage" includes, but the real kernel was still missing. Father had indicated if we wanted to know what our heritage was, we would discover it when we were old enough to understand.

Perhaps that time has come.

It may be helpful to back into the answer to his riddle by introducing a rather rare Norwegian term, *janteloven* (pronounced yahn'-teh-lohv-en). You may not find it in ordinary Norwegian-English dictionaries, but you will find it in a *Nynorsk* or country Norwegian dictionary such as *Ecolas Nynorsk Ordbok*. It is the so-called law that says, "you mustn't think you *are* anything." It warns you against holding too high an opinion of yourself. Call it the Norwegian law of imposed humility, which in exaggerated cases can be a destructive putdown. More naturally, it serves to remind Norwegians of the virtue of modesty and realistic self-appraisal.

As much as we saw of enforced humility elsewhere, in some American as well as in some Norwegian families, we didn't get that kind of abuse at home. No, very definitely, our treatment was quite the opposite. If anything, Gunnar hoped that we *would* become something, *be* something, and be aware of our own identity. Mother, too, wanted us to *be* something and used her utmost effort to dedicate us to that purpose. They both knew who and what they were, and they hoped we, too, would reach that sense of self-identity.

What Father and Mother would have thought had they

lived to see John as a United States Information Service officer and head of the Voice of America radio to occupied Europe during the Cold War! How delighted they were in Helga's acting, her appointment to the University of Washington teaching staff and her later success as a writer. They did not live to see their youngest son become a management consultant, but quite possibly that would not have surprised them, for as they often told us, "You come from good stock." By that they were not being racist, they were simply honoring their own parents and their country of origin. They were also implying that sustained effort toward excellence was expected of us.

Our parents were delighted to know that all three of us children had deep respect for Norway and treasured the special flavor and richness Norway and its traditions had given our lives. But what Mother and Father hoped most was that we would each find our life's work and perform it to the best of our abilities. They hoped we would do what they had done. *They wanted us to make something of our lives.* They set unmistakable examples for us.

They were not alone in setting these examples. If we had understood it at that time we could have seen many others who were following the same pattern. They were all around us in the Seattle where we grew up. They included many of the people who were Gunnar's subscribers and friends and Marie's willing co-workers in all the good works in which she was involved. There were many more of all national and racial origins.

Who were these people? Many were immigrants. Some had lived hard, difficult, sometimes disappointing lives, struggling to find their future in this land of promise. Most of them found it because they knew it was here and it was up to them to persevere, work and accomplish their goals. This they did without a government support system or a social safety net. They did it on their own, the way that counts.

They drove themselves. They took the long voyage. They endured the hunger, did the demanding work that hardens and shapes one and generates both competence and character. They eventually found their life work through which they became successful. In its deepest meaning, *they lived The American Dream.*

Is "The American Dream" dead? We are convinced it wasn't then. We know from our own lives that it isn't dead now. We lived it and many of our children and grandchildren are living it today.

If you have lived it, you can be sure your forebears nod their approval. They will say with pride, "These are our children. They too made the journey. They endured and learned to accept and honor the toil. They became Americans and they never forgot their heritage. They escaped the affliction of *janteloven*. They found their identities through repeating the core of the immigrant experience. They truly have become something."

We two aging offspring of Norwegian-American immigrants agree this is the "hidden heritage" Gunnar and Marie left us. We believe something quite similar is left to all the descendants of the immigrants from all nations. The crucial factor is not money, not an inheritance, *it is the heritage: the accepted challenge to replicate in our own lives the full meaning and reward of the immigrant experience in America. It is to live The American Dream.*

In today's America, still suffering scars of the negativism that exploded during the troubled sixties, "the American dream" is a badly tarnished concept. It was quite the opposite for the immigrants. They saw it as real. So do we. For we know that Gunnar and Marie believed it and proved it to be true. And so have we.

Would John have agreed with this interpretation of our mutual heritage? Of that we have no doubt. We are also sure Gunnar and Marie would be pleased that we finally discovered the answer to the heritage riddle.

Finding the meaning of our heritage is one reason why we embarked on the lengthy process and rewarding adventure of remembering and researching our family's past. This book is written not only to honor our parents, but also to realize who they really were, what they stood for, what they accomplished and, especially, what they expected us to achieve in our own lives by means of the special enduring heritage they bequeathed us.

We have called it an *enduring* heritage because it has survived and to indicate our faith that succeeding generations will also have reason to remember that their forebears came from Norway. May they enjoy and be enriched by their Norwegian heritage. We hope they will in their own lives experience the deep satisfaction of replicating the immigrant discovery of the American Dream. To quote Robert Pinsky, our American Poet Laureate, "deciding to remember, and what we remember, is how we decide what we are."

Sources

Files of *Washington Posten*, Seattle, WA, May 17, 1904 through May 17, 1944 - the source for most of the content of Chapters 5, 6, 8, 9, 10, and minor source for other chapters; by microfiche from Suzzalo Graduate Library, University of Washington, Seattle.

Western Viking (formerly *Washington Posten*), Seattle, WA, 100th anniversary issue May 17, 1989.

Dette Er Norge (This is Norway) book by Marie V. Lund, published by *Washington Posten*, Seattle, WA, Circa 1931.

Minner av Norge (Memories of Norway) article series by Marie V. Lund, in *Washington Posten* issues March 6 – May 22, 1931.

Incomplete and unpublished biography of Gunnar Lund by Marie V. Lund, undated but probably written in 1941.

Correspondence from Aslaug Wiggen Karterud, daughter of Anna Vognild Wiggen and niece of Marie Vognild Lund, various dates 1999.

Correspondence from Joan Taylor Lund and John Vognild Lund from Oslo, Norway to various members of the Taylor and Lund families, various dates 1947.

Unpublished Manuscript by John Vognild Lund and Joan Taylor Lund, *Norway and the Third Alternative,* written in 1947 in Norway. Manuscript now in custody of Scandinavian Heritage Museum, Seattle, WA.

Clippings from *Seattle Times* and *Seattle Post-Intelligencer,* various dates.

Interview notes from conversations with Erik Viken, Viken farm, Oppdal, Norway, 1936 and 1937.

Interview notes from conversations with Knut K. Dørum, Gulsenget farm, Oppdal, Norway 1936 and 1937.

Interview notes from conversations with John Vognild Lund, especially in 1991, High Point, NC.

Interview notes from personal conversations and innumerable telephone conversations with Helga Lund Parsons, Naples, FL and Greensboro, NC, 1991-2 and especially 1999 and 2000.

Interview notes from telephone conversations with Sheila Lund (widow of John V. Lund), Raleigh, NC, 1999 and 2000.

Telephone conversations with Laurel Keitel (daughter of John V. Lund), Minneapolis, MN, 2000.

Membership data from Sons of Norway, 1455 West Lake Street, Minneapolis, MN 55408, and the order's Viking Magazine centennial anniversary issue, January 1995.

Western Viking March 17, 2000, Article by Howard Olivers on District 2, Sons of Norway.

SOURCES

Computer Genealogies (unpublished):
David Denis, Winnetka, IL; Vognild
Herlaug Dørum, Trondheim, Norway; Dørum, Vognild, Viken
David R. Lund, Roseburg, OR; Vognild, Abrahamsen (Lund)
Rolf Erik Sanne, Stavanger, Norway; Abrahamsen (Lund)

Unpublished *Ytre Ustigard* (The Easternmost Farm) – A genealogy of the (Vognild) family on Ytre Ustigård (Vognild), by E. J. Engelsjord, (no date), Oppdal, translated and updated by Aslaug Wiggen Karterud, Trondheim, Norway.

Norwegian-American Historical Association books:
Concerning Our Heritage by Ole E. Rølvaag, translated from the Norwegian by Solveig Zempel, 1998.
Cultural Pluralism versus Assimilation, edited by Odd S. Lovoll, 1977
Ethnicity Challenged, by Carl H. Chrislock, 1981.
Immigrant Idealist; A Literary Biography of Waldemar Ager by Einar Haugen, 1989.
Norwegian-American Studies Volume 35,Pilgrimage and Propaganda: The Ameriacan Newspapermen's Tour of Norway in 1927, Terje I. Leiren.

Pomor; Nord-Norge og Nord-Russland Gjennom Tusen År (Pomor: North Norway and North Russia Through a Thousand Years), Einar Niemi (editor), Gyldendal Norsk Forlag, Oslo, 1992.

OUR ENDURING HERITAGE

Acknowledgements

Kathy Anderson, Portland, OR, Vesterheim *rosemaling* gold medalist for original pen-and-ink art used on chapter headings.

Kristin and Timothy Justice for their computer expertise and many hours of work in preparing the manuscript for publishing.

Laurel Keitel, Minneapolis, MN for photographs of John Lund.

Ilamae Lund for invaluable help in copy and proof reading.

Sheila Lund for photograph of John Lund.

Scandinavian Heritage Museum, Seattle WA for photographs of Gunnar Lund.

Bruce M. Beaton, Photographer, for his inspired photo of the very old red trunk.